Jack went to sea when he was 17, as a newly qualified Radio Operator. It was 1919, just after the end of the First World War. There were still a few mines floating about.

They didn't hit any mines, but they did hit bottom a few times and had trouble with ice, fog, gales and fires. All part of the routine life, jobbing around the world for the best part of two decades, delivering cargo in a series of ships.

They were small ships by modern standards, mainly driven by steam piston engines, fuelled by coal and not very fast. Cargo was often in bags, loaded and unloaded by hand. A slow process made even slower if cargo had to be ferried to or from shore in lighters.

Jack kept a log - where they started, what the cargo was, where they were and when. It's dispassionate but every now and then the going was obviously tricky. This book quotes from the log and draws from it, to get a feel for what life was like, what the sea was like and what shipping was like, all those years ago.

NOVELS
BY
KENNETH HODGKIN

Needing to Know !

A Better Mousetrap

JACK'S LOG

All at Sea
in the
1920s and 30s

Kenneth Hodgkin

ISBN 978-0-9873587-4-5

Layout, Cover Design and Publication by:

Ken Hodgkin
Design
Writing

A catalogue record for this
book is available from the
NATIONAL
LIBRARY   National Library of Australia
OF AUSTRALIA

Publisher: Kenneth Hodgkin
Title: Jack's Log - All at Sea in the 1920s & 30s
Author: Kenneth Hodgkin.
ISBN: 9780987358745 (pbk.)

This is for Jack, whose log it is. I remember him with enormous affection and he died far too young. And it is for his descendents, over a dozen at the last count, and for anybody else interested by life at sea nearly a hundred years ago.

April 1919

Writer's Note

Jack Hodgkin was my father. He died over fifty years ago and I'm quite a bit older now than the age he reached. I was always aware, when growing up, that he had spent most of his young adult life at sea. He didn't make a big thing about it but he had a few stories about his sailor pals being daft when full of whisky.

Judging by his expenses lists, he probably had a fair bit of whisky himself!

It's my good fortune that he kept a log of his time at sea. For many years I thought it was quite limited but then I found another trove of notebooks. I've enjoyed myself going through them, extracting exciting bits, getting a feel for some of the dull routine and time spent waiting for cargoes and in getting them on and off ships. And I've enjoyed using the log, together with a few photos and maps, to form this book.

I hope you find it as interesting as I did.

Kenneth Hodgkin
November 2017

CONTENTS

Maps

Photographs

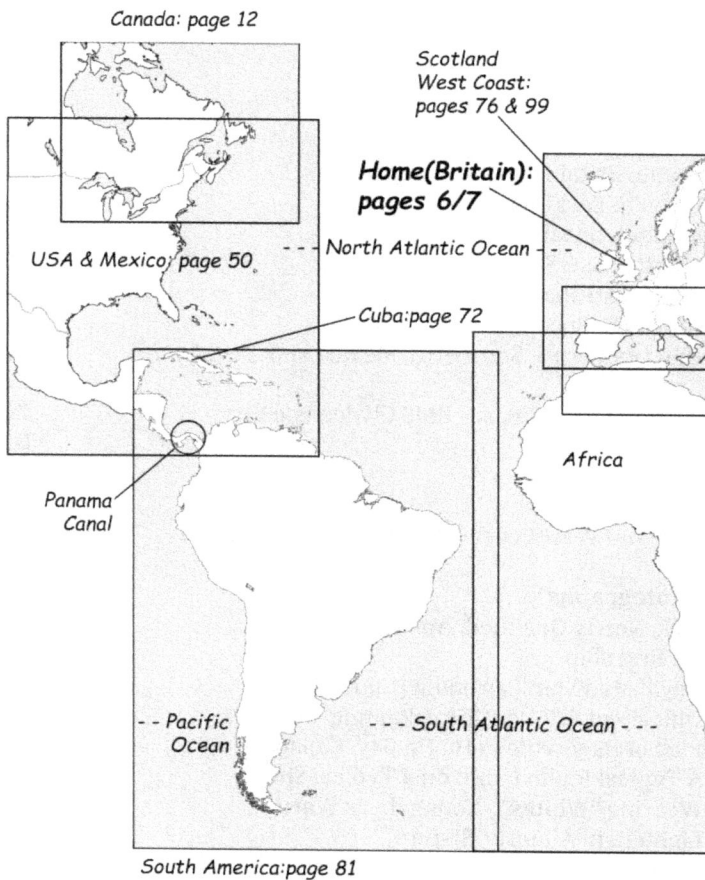

Canada: page 12

Scotland
West Coast:
pages 76 & 99

Home(Britain):
pages 6/7

USA & Mexico: page 50 --- North Atlantic Ocean ---

Cuba: page 72

Africa

Panama
Canal

-- Pacific   --- South Atlantic Ocean ---
Ocean

South America: page 81

Composite of the maps interspersed through this book
- for voyages to the west and south

x

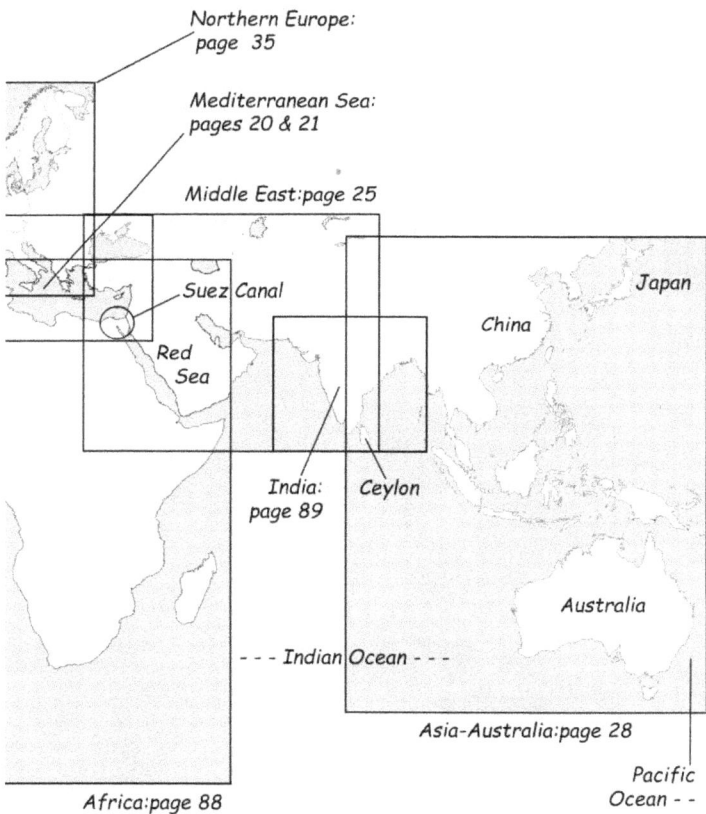

Northern Europe:
page 35

Mediterranean Sea:
pages 20 & 21

Middle East:page 25

Suez Canal

Japan

China

Red
Sea

India:
page 89

Ceylon

Australia

- - - Indian Ocean - - -

Asia-Australia:page 28

Pacific
Ocean - -

Africa:page 88

- and for voyages predominantly east and south
  via the Mediterranean Sea or west coast of Africa

Jargon

Jack used some nautical terms.
Meanings and Measures on pages 143 - 146 explains these and other things that might seem a little obscure.

1. Building Up Steam

Jack, my father, John Coulton Hodgkin to give him his formal name, grew up in a tiny village at the southern edge of the English Lake District. He was born in 1901, an only child. He and his parents lived in a rented house and, when he became an adult, this continued to be "home" until he got married and had a home of his own.

Tiny though the village was, it had a railway station, a junction no less. A single track branch line went to Coniston and the main line went to just about anywhere you wanted. This turned out to be very useful in Jack's adult life.

As a small boy, he went to the school in the next village, about a mile away. My guess is that he usually walked but, maybe if the weather was bad, he would take the branch line train. There was no question of him being delivered and collected by car as happens so much today. It wasn't common to have a car back then and his parents never did have a car.

On the other hand it wasn't common back then to be paranoid about the safety of children wandering around on their own. A simpler, more straightforward time in many ways. But then, only a little later, the First World War started - the sort of simple straightforwardness that can well be done without.

When older, and when the war was on, Jack went to the Grammar School in Ulverston, travelling by train every day round the tip of the Furness Peninsula. Many years later I lived in the same tiny village and went to the same Grammar School - though it was in a new building by then. There was no luxurious train ride for me! I had to travel in a stinky bus full of smoking farmers, going over the moors with all their ups and downs and twists and turns. Many was the time I had to stop the bus when motion sickness struck. I envied my Dad that train.

Jack would probably have been fine on my stinky bus. He didn't suffer from motion sickness. If he did, he never mentioned it. Or else it must have been knocked out of him when he went to sea. Because go to sea he did.

There were no 'O' and 'A' level exams at the end of school back then. Instead, you were tested on a range of subjects and, if you passed, you "matriculated". Jack passed.

His time of leaving school pretty much coincided with the end of the First World War. Going to University was much less common then than it is now and he didn't have a mind-set to do that anyway. He wanted to be up and off, not messing about. If the war had still been on, he would have joined in. But it wasn't, so he went to sea in the merchant navy.

Around the turn of the century, so less than twenty years before, Guglielmo Marconi had made the first successful long distance radio communication, across the Atlantic. Marconi developed his techniques and equipment further and went on to establish the Marconi Company. Among other things, this company employed specialist wireless telegraphers for communications at sea. These were the "Marconi Men", the Wireless Operators assigned to ships. They were commonly known as "Sparks".

Jack left school in 1918. He trained as a Marconi Man and, in February 1919, still aged 17, got his certificate. Formally, he was then a Wireless Telegraphy Operator.

That's a Radio Officer in today's terms. It was cutting-edge, hi-tech stuff at the time.

We might not think it now. Transmission in the early days was by generating sparks between two metal balls. Messages were sent and received in Morse Code (dots and dashes). Bandwidth at the time was anything but broad.

With this qualification under his belt, Jack signed up to go to sea in merchant ships. He went from ship to ship, depending on who needed a Wireless Operator at the time he was available. Sometimes he stayed on a ship for several voyages, sometimes he swapped ships after only a short time. The voyages nearly all started and finished in Britain - England, Scotland or Wales - and he used that very handy railway station at home to get to and from the various ports.

Jack kept a log of his voyages - where they started, what the cargo was, where they passed and when. At first, he kept a neat copy and that was all I knew about. But then I discovered the originals, in little notebooks - one of them was from a laundry in Paisley, Scotland, meant for listing the items sent for cleaning. Waste not, want not!

Apart from one short, missing gap the notebooks covered all his years at sea. He apparently got fed up after a few years with keeping the neat copy, the rough originals being sufficient for his personal records. They were a bit harder to read but quite a find.

The log is always dispassionate and largely routine but, now and then, the going was obviously challenging.

It starts just after the First World War. It isn't about fighting or derring do, just the job of moving cargo around the world in ships that, by today's standards, were small and slow. A job which had its moments and its interesting asides.

The entire handwritten log still exists in its note books but I thought it would make it more accessible to outline the voyages and to highlight the entries which were clearly not routine. I have also been able, for most of the ships, to find a few details - when built, how big and how powered. They were all (except one) steam ships: nearly all had piston engines and relied on coal as fuel.

It has also been pretty educational for me to find out where the ports and places are on a map (or were in some cases, names having changed). Some of the place names took a bit of hunting down. My favourite was Queenstown. Leaving Canada to cross the Atlantic and deliver a cargo to Hamburg, they ran into rough weather which chewed up more fuel than they had allowed for. So there's a note when off Cape Race (the eastern tip of Newfoundland) that they will divert to Queenstown for bunkers (i.e a refuelling stop). Well there's a Queenstown in Ontario but that didn't make sense and one in New Zealand which made even less sense. Finally, I discovered Queenstown had been the name of Cobh in Eira, on the south coast of Ireland - on Cork Harbour. It had been renamed Queenstown in honour of a visit there by Queen Victoria. Not an honour that Eire would want to maintain, so it has since gone back to its old name and that particular Queenstown isn't on modern maps. However, it *was* en route from Newfoundland to Hamburg with very little diversion, so they got the extra fuel they needed.

Just an aside about the maps in this book - they aren't the sort you could use for navigation! They are just meant to give a reasonable idea of where the various ports are or were. The thickness of a line or a slight shift to make things fit amounts to many a mile when you scale it up. I also have to confess that geography has never been my strong point. I found that locating ports and placing them on a map improved my knowledge greatly - but the more geographically astute might find errors. If so, they are mine.

I started off using the log pretty much unchanged. Then, having got the flavour of long spells at sea, with every headland noteworthy, I became more selective. Later again, I found myself summarising more and more, using direct log extracts only where conditions became exciting. Bits in square brackets are my interjections. There are also linking passages and commentary that is obviously mine and not from the log.

You can also blame me for putting stuff in bold if I thought it sufficiently out of the routine to warrant extra attention - the original is more laconic, with all events just being part of the day's work. "Nowt to go on about," Jack might well have said.

So, just as Jack's log evolved from comprehensive neatness to comprehensive but ever more tiny script, so has the style of this book evolved on the way from beginning to end.

It's probably best dipped into a few pages at a time and in no particular order, rather than being a solid, front to back read. But that's up to you and how you find it.

Jack stayed at sea until September 1937. A few years before then, when assigned to a Macbrayne's ship (my best guess is 1931 on SS Lochbroom) operating round the Scottish Islands and carrying paying passengers, he met his wife to be, and my mother to be, enjoying a cruise on board. She had been widowed a couple of years before, had gone back to live in Sunderland, where she grew up, and was about to start training as a nurse in Newcastle-on-Tyne. I think her father had treated her to the trip. It turned out to be a very good treat: she and Jack married on New Years' Day 1938.

Some of the entries in the log make me realise that Jack's survival to the time of that meeting was not a sure thing. The meeting itself was one of those happy crossings of random paths. My own existence is one of its results.

I'm very pleased that fate allowed that meeting, and therefore me, to happen.

The map opposite, of most of the British Isles, shows the approximate locations of the ports Jack's ships left from and returned to. The rivers shown have several port locations within them, too detailed to fit on the map, so listed below.

"Home" on the southern edge of the Lake District is Foxfield, the tiny village where Jack grew up and where his parents continued to live (and where we lived as a family later in his life.) Tiny or not, it had a railway station which was obviously of great help in getting to and from home ports.

River Tay
DUNDEE, Tayport

River Clyde
GLASGOW, Clydeside,
Greenock, Bowling, Renfrew

River Forth
EDINBURGH/Granton
Grangemouth, Burntisland

River Mersey
LIVERPOOL, Birkenhead,
Manchester (via Ship Canal)

River Tyne
NEWCASTLE-ON-TYNE,
SOUTH SHIELDS, Gateshead,
Hebbern-on-Tyne, Jarrow,
Wallsend-on-Tyne, Pelaw,
Dunstan-on-Tyne, Tyne Dock

River Severn
SWANSEA, CARDIFF/Penarth,
Barry, Newport, Sharpness,
Avonmouth, Portishead

River Medway
Queensborough

River Thames
LONDON/Tilbury, Gravesend
Dagenham, Purfleet

West Hartlepool is on the east coast of England, between the River Tyne and Middlesborough.

Wearmouth/Wearmouth Staithes is at Sunderland.

Home: Main Rivers and Ports of Call in Britain

2. Weighing Anchor

As a seventeen year old, fresh out of Grammar School, Jack put his name on his logbook and began with his new qualifications and first allocated ship. His first appointment only lasted five days and he didn't leave port because he was transferred to S.S. War - Timiskaming, a new ship nearing completion in Canada.

1919.

FEB 20TH 1919. - Obtained P.M.G.'s 1ST Class Certificate in Wireless Telegraphy.

APRIL 16TH - Joined Marconi I.M.C. Co., at Newcastle-on-Tyne.

APRIL 17TH - Appointed 2nd Operator to S.S. "BLAIRMORE", lying in Tyne Dock.

APRIL 22ND - Transferred from "BLAIRMORE".

APRIL 23RD - Appointed 2nd Oper. to S.S. "WAR TIMISKAMING", building at Toronto, Ont.

3. First Adventure

Maps: Home(Britain):pages 6/7   Canada:page 12

I reckon this must have been quite an exciting start for a young lad leaving home for the first time so haven't abridged it. Occasional emphases are mine. There are surprising gaps of time at the start, a week between appointment and signing articles and another three weeks before setting off:

1919	**S/S War-Timiskaming, of London**
	(Owners - The Well Line) Voyage No. 1
	[Canadian ports, returning to England]
May 1 (Thu)	Signed articles at Newcastle on Tyne.
May 21 (Wed)	4.00pm Left LIVERPOOL on the "Carmania", for Halifax NS, in company with the other officers of the "War Timiskaming" to go overland from Halifax to Toronto, to join the ship. 1st Class expenses paid throughout.

RMS Carmania

May 22	5.00am Passed the TUSKAR ROCK.
(Thu)	Weather rather bad to the Fastnet, but very good afterwards. Thick fog on the Newfoundland Banks.
May 28	Arrived HALIFAX NS.
(Wed)	Disembarked at Halifax. Stayed at the Queens Hotel. Left Halifax at 7.40am on the 29th and went overland to Toronto, via Quebec and Montreal.

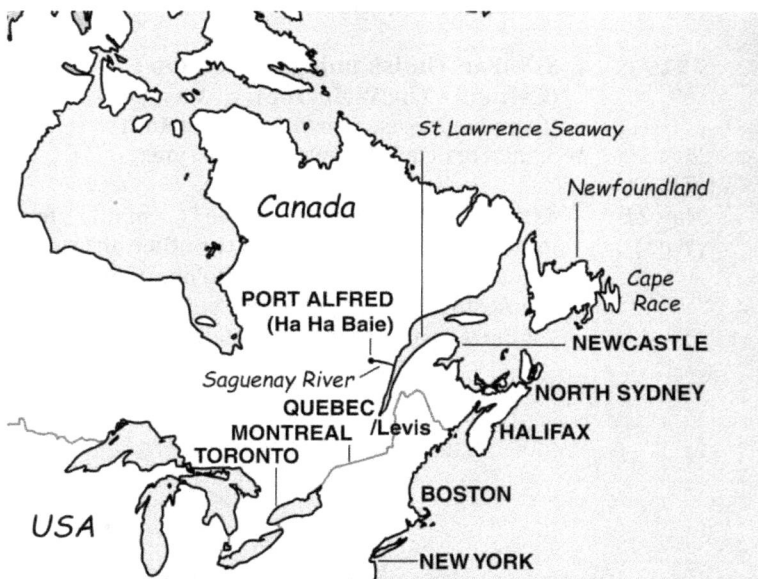

East Coast of Canada, bordering on USA

| May 30 | 6.00am Arrived TORONTO. |
| (Fri) | S/S "War Timiskaming" lying at Polson's Ironworks, not quite completed. Put up at the Walker House Hotel, Toronto, waiting for the ship. Trial trip took place on Lake Ontario on Sunday, June 1st. Went out to Niagara Falls on June 4th. |

June 5 (Thu)	4.00pm Left TORONTO. Light ship, bound Montreal.
	Builder's crew taking ship down to Montreal.
June 6 (Fri)	2.00pm Arrived PRESCOTT.
	Put Polson's Directors ashore here.
	4.00pm Left PRESCOTT.
June 7 (Sat)	4.00pm Arrived MONTREAL.
	Went into Montreal Dry Dock on June 10th, for ship to be completed. In dry dock until the 17th. Came out on that date into the Lachine Canal Basin, near the Grand Trunk Elevator. Tank bottoms pitched, and finishing touches put on vessel. Vessel ready for sea on June 30th. Moved down to coal tips on that date, and bunkered. Very hot weather all this time.
July 1 (Tue)	5.30am Left MONTREAL, light ship, bound Quebec.
	7.30pm Arrived QUEBEC.
	Went into the Louise Tidal Basin, and loaded part cargo of logs as ballast. Went out to Montmorency Falls on July 4th.
July 5 (Sat)	5.30am Left QUEBEC, bound Newcastle NB.
	10.30am Passed FATHER POINT. Dropped the pilot.
July 6	3.00pm Passed FAME POINT.
	8.00pm Abeam of POINT GASPE.
	Touched bottom at entrance to Miramanchi Bay, at 6.00am on July 7th. **Dropped anchor immediately and sent to Newcastle for pilot.** Pilot aboard about 4.00pm.
July 7 (Mon)	9.30pm Arrived NEWCASTLE NB.
	Anchored on the river overnight, and went alongside at daybreak. Finished loading with deals, taking a nine foot deck cargo. Total cargo 3000 tons. **("War Tamiskaming" was the second steamer to go to Newcastle since the outbreak of war)**
July 16 (Wed)	3.45pm Left NEWCASTLE NB, bound North Sydney CB.
	Dense fog all the way.

July 18	11.00am Arrived NORTH SYDNEY CB.
(Fri)	Took in bunkers and fresh water.
July 19	4.30am Left NORTH SYDNEY CB, bound Brow
(Sat)	Head, Ireland, for orders **(Peace Celebration Day). Engine trouble developed soon after leaving Sydney. Ship stopped for 12 hours, 100 miles east of Sydney. Stopped again several times on way across. Dense fog again on the Banks of Newfoundland. Keeping well to the south of Cape Race, on account of fog and ice.** Wireless orders received from Valencia on July 30th, to proceed to Barrow-in-Furness to discharge.
July 30	9.00pm Passed the FASTNET.
(Wed)	
July 31	2.00pm Rounded the TUSKAR ROCK.
(Thu)	11.00pm Off HOLYHEAD.
Aug 1	3.30am Arrived BARROW-IN-FURNESS.
(Fri)	Berthed in Buccleuch Dock, and discharged cargo at Crossfields Wharf. End of Voyage. Home on leave Aug 1st - 14th. Rejoined "War Timiskaming" at Barrow, 9.00am Aug 14th.

That first voyage took exactly three months from start to finish. By a nice coincidence it ended in Barrow, only a few miles from Jack's home.

Taken on S/S War Timiskaming 1919

4. Routine - and Mines, Strikes and Storms

Maps: Home(Britain):pages 6/7 Mediterranean:pages 20/21

Voyage 2 was very short, from 14 - 18 August 1919. It took S/S War Timiskaming from Barrow to Cardiff.

Aug 18	10.00am Arrived CARDIFF.
(Mon)	Went into Mount Stuart Dry Dock for overhaul and repairs. Ship sold to the French. End of Voyage. Home on leave Aug 22 - 28. Returned to Cardiff Aug 28, and appointed 2nd Operator to S/S "Newquay".

S/S Newquay 30 Aug 1919 to 9 Nov 1919 [10 weeks]: from Cardiff (carrying 7000 tons of coal) to Mediterranean ports: Ancona [Italy], Sebenico [now Sibinek, Croatia], La Goulette [Tunisia], Oran [Algeria], Mazarron [Spain], Gibraltar and home to Middlesborough [North-East England].

S/S Newquay
Built 1914
Gross Registered Tonnage 4207
Length 370 feet
Beam 51 feet
Horse Power 386: Steam driven piston engine, coal fuelled.

Sep 9	6.00am Abeam of CAPE S. VITO (Sicily).
(Tue)	**Steering to the north of Sicily on account of drifting mines to the south.**
Sep 10	3.00pm Rounded CAPE S. MARIA DI LEUCA.
(Wed)	**Many floating mines still adrift in the Adriatic, so proceeding up the coast at half speed.**
Sep 13	9.00am Arrived ANCONA.
(Sat)	Discharged 6,300tons of coal. **Men working cargo went on strike in sympathy with the**

railwaymen, after discharging this amount. **Strike took place on 23rd.** 700 tons of coal still remaining on board. Orders received to proceed to Sebenico, to discharge remainder.

Sep 24 (Wed)
6.30am Left ANCONA bound Sebenico, Dalmatia. 8.00pm Arrived SEBENICO.
Went alongside quay and discharged remaining 700tons of coal. **Italian troops in occupation of town.**

......

Oct 13 (Mon)
6.45pm Left ORAN, light ship, bound Mazarron, Spain.
Rough passage to Mazarron. Moderate beam sea and strong wind. Ship rolling heavily.

Oct 14 (Tue)
7.45am Arrived MAZARRON.
Anchored half a mile from the shore and loaded full cargo (7000 tons) of iron ore from lighters. Moderate wind and sea on 28th and 29th. **Vessel rolling and hindering the loading. Loading stopped altogether for some hours, as lighters unable to get alongside.**

......

Oct 31 (Fri)
8.00am Arrived GIBRALTAR.
Anchored in the bay for bunkers. **Unable to obtain them as men on shore are all on strike.**
Took in fresh water and stores.
1.30pm Left GIBRALTAR, bound Middlesborough.

Nov 1 (Sat)
3.00pm Rounded CAPE ST VINCENT. Fairly heavy swell, increasing rapidly.

Nov 2 (Sun)
1.00am Passed CAPE ROCA. Sea getting worse. Ship rolling heavily.

Nov 3 (Mon)
6.00am Off FINISTERE.
Sea now very rough. Tremendous wind and sea in Bay of Biscay. Ship rolling terribly. Driven out of our course to a point 150 miles to the westward of Ushant.

Nov 6 (Thu)	2.00am Passed USHANT. Weather now moderating. Much better in the channel, but foggy.
Nov 7 (Fri)	7.00pm In the STRAITS OF DOVER. Bad weather begins again. **Sea very rough. Several ships ashore in the Channel and on the East Coast.** Arrived off the mouth of the Tees at 4.00am on the 9th, and stood off and on, waiting for a pilot, but **sea too rough for cutter to come out**. Pilot aboard eventually at 4.00pm, though wind and sea increasing again.
Nov 9 (Sun)	5.00pm arrived MIDDLESBOROUGH.
Nov 19 (Tue)	signed off at Middlesborough [after 10 days in port].

End of Voyage.
Home on leave Nov 20th - Dec 1st.

Returned to Newcastle on Dec 1st and appointed to
S/S "Massis" the following day.
"Massis" lying at Hawthorne, Leslie's Dry Dock, Hebburn-on-Tyne.
Appointed 1st Operator.

So that's progress - First Operator now, not Second.

It's interesting how much time they sometimes spent in port.
They arrived in Mazarron on October 14 and were still loading from lighters about two weeks later, before leaving for Gibraltar.
   And there were ten days between arriving in Middlesborough and signing off for the end of the voyage. Not like todays' container ships.

Atlantic Ocean

Ushant

Bay of Biscay

Finisterre

BILBAO

MARSEILLES
TOULON
SAVONA
GENOA
LA SPEZIA

BURRIANA
VALENCIA
GANDIA

ALICANTE
TORRE VEIJA
CARTEGANA
MAZARRON
AGUILAS
GARRUCHA
CARBONERAS
ALMERIA

LISBON
Cape
St Vincent
HUELVA
SEVILLE
GIBRALTAR

Gulf of Lions

LEGHORN
(Livorno)

NAPLES

IVICA
(Ibiza)

PORTO FERRAGO
(Island of Elba)

ORAN
&
ARZEW

ALGIERS

BONE

BIZERTE
&
TUNIS

LA GOLETTE

West Mediterranean Sea bordering on Spain, France, Italy and North Africa

ANCONA
SEBENICO (Sibinek)
Black Sea
BATOUM
CONSTANTINOPLE
AUGUSTA (Sicily)
PIREAUS (Athens)
Mediterranean Sea
PORT SAID
Suez Canal
ALEXANDRIA

East Mediterranean (and Aegean) Sea bordering Italy, Croatia, Greece, Turkey, North Africa/Egypt and the entrance to the Suez Canal

5. Long Trip to Everywhere
- a bit of tension ashore

Maps: Home(Britain):pages 6/7   USA:page 50
Mediterranean:pages 20/21   Middle East:page 25
Asia-Australia:page 28

S/S Massis 6 Dec 1919 to 5 Jan 1921 [13 months]:
The voyage started with a trip to New Orleans (USA) to collect cargo, then it took in Mediterranean ports and continued through the Suez Canal to Iraq, Ceylon (now Sri Lanka), Indonesia, Japan, China, Borneo, Australia (Adelaide, Melbourne and Sydney) and Singapore. There was a second lap of the last three then directly home via the Suez Canal.

In more detail it went from Hebburn-on-Tyne, light to New Orleans, then Lisbon, Spezia, Augusta, Constantinople [now Istanbul], Batoum [now Batumi, Georgia], Constantinople, Alexandria, Port Said, Suez, Abadan [Persian Gulf], Colombo, Pulo Bukom [now part of Singapore], Pulo Samboe, Kobe, Taketoyo, Shanghai, Balikpapan [Borneo], Adelaide, Melbourne, Sydney NSW, Singapore, Pulo Samboe, Pladjoe, Singapore, Melbourne, Sydney, Balikpapan, Adelaide, Melbourne, Sydney (lightly loaded), Balikpapan, Singapore, Suez, Port Said and home to Portishead [on the River Severn, west coast of England].

S/S Massis
Built 1914
Gross registered Tonnage 5022
Length 385 feet
Beam 50 feet
Horse Power 425: Steam driven piston engine, coal fuelled.

The voyage started with no cargo but she loaded and discharged the likes of kerosene, distillate, benzine and similar liquids at ports along the way.

Dec 8	3.00am. Passed CAPE WRAITH.
(Mon)	**Weather bad till about the 20th. Ship pitching and rolling heavily, and shipping much water.** Weather afterwards improves gradually and gets much warmer.
1920	
Jan 1	9.00am arrived NEW ORLEANS.
(Thu)	... loaded 6000tons of kerosene (paraffin) in 13 hours 50 minutes pumping time, **creating a record for New Orleans [!]**
.....	
Jan 4	10.00pm Crossed the SOUTH PASS BAR of the
(Sun)	Mississippi. **... Dirty weather to Key West. Shipping heavy water.**
.....	
Feb 1	3.00pm Off CAPE SAN SEBASTIAN.
(Sun)	**... Very bad weather experienced in the Gulf of Lions [Mediterranean Sea]. Strong gale and heavy sea. Ship rolling heavily and taking much water** ... fine again next morning.
.....	
Feb 8	3.00am Arrived off Augusta but sea too rough to
(Sun)	go inside, so lay off and on until 5.00pm and then entered the harbour and anchored. Went alongside the following morning and finished discharging.
.....	
Feb 15	1.30pm Left CONSTANTINOPLE for Batoum.
(Sun)	4.30pm Entered the BLACK SEA. Weather was much colder, and country covered with snow. Arrived off Batoum at 8.00pm on the 17th and cruised about all night **(part of the time unknowingly on a minefield).**
Feb 18	7.45am Arrived BATOUM.
(Wed)	... took in full cargo of kerosene and distillate. Distillate (2100tons) had been used for cleaning out the pipeline from Baku to Batoum when it was reopened after the armistice. **Bolsheviks**

now lively in the district, and advancing towards Batoum. **Several soldiers killed by snipers in Batoum.**

.....

Feb 26 (Thu)	6.00am Left CONSTANTINOPLE for Alexandria. **Italian oil tank on fire in the Sea of Marmora.** ...

.....

Mar 1 (Mon)	5.00am Arrived ALEXANDRIA. ... Discharged the kerosene (4500tons). **Arabs are in a state almost bordering on revolution. The native quarters of the town are unsafe at night, many white men being murdered.**

.....

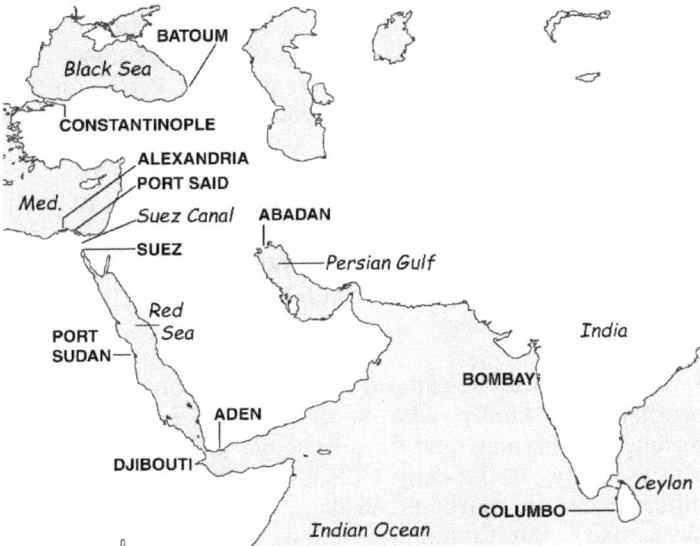

Middle East: Suez Canal Eastward

Mar 23 (Tue)	1.30pm Arrived ABADAN. Anchored in midstream overnight. Went alongside the following morning and loaded with kerosene down to 19 feet. Impossible to load deeper as there is only 20ft of water on the bar.
Mar 29 (Mon)	11.30am Left ABADAN. 5.30pm Crossed the bar of the SHAT-EL-ARAB. Anchored outside the Bar. Lay at anchor doing nothing till April 4th. Then completed loading from lighters. Extremely hot weather.
.....	
June 6 (Sun)	5.30am Left BALIKPAPAN bound Adelaide, Australia. **Three coolie stowaways found, three hours after leaving. Turned back and put them aboard the lightship.**

Many decades later, Jayne and I moved to Perth, Western Australia, for what we thought was a three year stint. But we then started a family and have lived in Perth ever since. Jack didn't call in at Fremantle (the port town for Perth) on this voyage but it gave me a pang to read the various local place names he passed on this leg:

June 16 (Wed)	00.45am Off CAPE NATURALIST [in the SW near Margaret River]. 6.00am Off CAPE LEEUWIN [ditto]. 11.30am Off CAPE D'ENTRECASTEAUX [on the south coast].

Sydney is a place I've enjoyed visiting - sometimes to see my brother and family who settled there, sometimes for business, sometimes just for a holiday. Jack's voyages took him to Sydney in the early 1920s. It would have been very different - no Harbour Bridge, no Opera House, no skyscrapers. But it's still nice to think of him walking around the same city centre streets I've walked around.

June 21	6.45pm Arrived PORT ADELAIDE ...
(Mon)	
June 25	7.00am Left PORT ADELAIDE, bound Melbourne.
(Fri)	
June 26	3.00pm Off CAPE NELSON.
(Sat)	**Passed HMS Renown, with the Prince of Wales on board, about midnight on the 26th, bound Albany from Sydney.**
	[Albany is on the south coast of Western Australia and now a favourite holiday spot. It is where most of the Australian troops set sail for Gallipoli in the First World War.]

.....

July 3	00.15am
(Sat)	Arrived SYDNEY NSW. Anchored off Garden Island overnight. Went alongside at British Imperial Oil Co's [now BP] wharf at Gore Cove, Greenwich ...
July 8	4.00pm Left SYDNEY, bound Singapore.
(Thu)	

.....

July 15	7.45pm Anchored for the night in NEWCASTLE
(Thu)	BAY.
	Numerous unlit islands make night navigation impossible. Under way again shortly after daybreak on the 16th.
July 27	8.00am Arrived SINGAPORE.
(Tue)	... Went into King's Dry Dock, Keppel Harbour at 9.30am on the 28th. Ship scraped and painted. Out of dry dock at 9.00am on 30th.
July 30	10.00am left SINGAPORE bound Pulo Samboe
(Fri)	(and then PLADJOE, Sumatra).
Aug 1	8.30pm Arrived PLADJOE.
(Sun)	... loaded part cargo of benzine (3000 tons).
	Unable to load to more than 19 feet owing to shallowness of water at river bar.
Aug 4	3.30pm Left PLADJOE, bound Singapore.
(Wed)	**Ran into river bank at 4.15pm and remained there until tide backed up at 6.30.**

.....

Asia-Australia
- east from India to Asian and Australian Ports

Sep 28	6.30am Left BALIKPAPAN, bound Adelaide.
(Tue)	... North-West Cape ... Cape Naturaliste ... Cape Leeuwin ... Adelaide.
	... Melbourne ... Sydney ... Thursday Island ... Balikpapan ... Singapore ... Suez ... Port Said.
Dec 18	9.00pm Left PORT SAID, bound Portishead.
(Sat)	Dec 22nd at 11.00am, **fire breaks out aft, in stokehold, some oil fuel being accidentally ignited. Oil shut off at bunker feed-pipes but unable to get at stokehold with extinguishers. Ship turned head to wind and stopped until fire burns out in about an hour. Considerable damage done below but vessel able to proceed.**

.....

Dec 31	2.30am Off CAPE FINISTERRE.
(Fri)	**Heavy sea and strong gale across Bay of Biscay** ...
1921	
Jan 2	6.00am Abeam of SCILLY ISLES.
(Sun)	Passing outside on account of bad weather.
Jan 5 wed	Docked at PORTISHEAD.
	Signed off Jan 6.
	End of voyage.

Home on leave Jan 6th - Feb 24th [a good spell of leave after more than a year at sea].
Appointed to **S/S "Gyp"** at Cardiff on Feb 28th as Operator in Charge.

6. Rock and Roll, with Ice

Maps: Home(Britain):pages 6/7   Mediterranean:pages 20/21
Canada:page 12

S/S Gyp 2 Mar 1921 to 14 May 1921 [about 10 weeks]:
Initially to the Mediterranean then across the Atlantic to Canada and back.

Ports: from Cardiff (Wales) to Naples (Italy), Torrevieja (Spain), Gibraltar, Halifax NS (Nova Scotia, Canada) and home to Aberdeen (east coast of Scotland).

S/S Gyp
Built 1905
Gross Registered Tonnage 3338
Length 340 feet
Beam 48 feet
Horse Power 308: Steam driven piston engine, coal fuelled.

To give a little more technical information (S/S Gyp was broadly typical of most of Jack's ships):
Single screw, driven by a triple expansion engine with cylinders of 24" [about 0.6 metres], 40" and 65" [i.e a steam driven piston engine with three cylinders - high pressure, intermediate pressure and low pressure: cylinder diameter getting bigger as steam pressure to be handled gets lower. As the log shows, they had to repair a cracked high pressure cylinder on one voyage.]

All cylinders had a 45" stroke. Boiler pressure was 180 psi (pounds per square inch, so about 12 times atmospheric pressure). A modern power station uses pressures of around 2400 psi.

Horse Power at 308, was around the same power as a modern inter-city bus.

Mar 2	1.30pm Left CARDIFF, bound Naples.
(Wed)	Full cargo (5000 tons) of coal and patent fuel.
Mar 3	8.00am Passed the LONGSHIPS.
(Thu)	60 miles west of Ushant at 6.00pm. Moderate beam swell, and **ship rolling heavily**. Very cold.
Mar 12	11.45am Arrived NAPLES.
(Sat)	... Went alongside on 13th at 9.30am, then onto the coal wharf. ...began discharging on 14th, and finished at 6.00pm on 18th [very slow process in today's terms].
Mar 18	6.30pm Leaving NAPLES (light ship), bound
(Fri)	Torreveija (Spain) ....
Mar 19	11.15pm Off CAPE SPARTIVENTO (Sardinia).
(Sat)	Sea slight **but ship rolling heavily.**
Mar 22	5.30am arrived TORREVEIJA.
(Tue)	Started loading cargo 23rd after lime washing holds. Loaded full cargo of salt (about 5000 tons) from lighters - at anchor in the bay.
Mar 26	4.00pm Leaving TORREVEIJA, bound Gibraltar
(Sat)	(for bunkers and fresh water).
.....	
Mar 28	1.00am Leaving GIBRALTAR, bound Halifax NS.
(Mon)	**Rolling heavily to the Azores. Rough weather. Shipping heavy water.**
Apr 2	3.00pm Passing S.MIGUEL (Azores).
(Sat)	Weather moderating **but still rolling heavily.**
Apr 8 & 9	**Very bad weather. Rolling very heavily and shipping water over lower bridge. Starboard jollyboat carried away and stove in. Rolling up to 45 degrees at times and in danger of foundering. At 3.00am on 8th took roll in excess of 50 degrees. Terrific weather. Vessel hove to.** Weather moderates on 10th. **Dense fog from then onwards.**
Apr 13	3.00am Arrived HALIFAX NS.
(Wed)	7.00am began discharging cargo... 6.00am 15th moved to ... continued discharging ... 6.00am

18th moved to ... completed discharging - 6.00am 23rd moved to Pier 3 and commenced loading paper pulp ...

Apr 29 (Fri) 9.00pm Left HALIFAX NS, bound Aberdeen.

May 2 (Mon) 8.30am Abeam of CAPE RACE (Newfoundland). **At 2.30am May 3rd encountered very heavy field ice with many bergs and growlers. Vessel going dead slow all day through ice. At 11.00am bent some of the bow plates. At 4.30pm tore hole in vessel's bow. Making water rapidly. Aft ballast tanks pumped up and vessel tipped by the stern, placing hole above level of water. Propellor also damaged at this time. Vessel stopped all night. Unable return to St John's NF owing to probability of imminent bad weather and consequent danger of returning through ice field, eighty miles in width.**

Proceeded next morning, May 4th, in good weather and ran clear of field ice in about one hour.

Damage now found to extend below water line. On May 8th encountered bad weather. No. 1 hold making water. On May 9th, No. 2 hold also making water. Water gaining very rapidly on pumps. At 3.00pm, May 9th, proceeded to jettison cargo from foredeck and No 1 hold. Water gained 3 feet in half an hour this afternoon in No.1.

Weather moderates again during night, but increases on May 10th. Water still gaining and now impossible to jettison more cargo owing to increasing weather.

Prepared to abandon ship during night (May 10th) but established communication with Swedish S/S Drottningholm so hung on. Morning of May 11th pumps began to gain on

water - pulp probably swelled and partially checked inflow. Vessel - previously several feet down by the head and almost out of control - slowly righting herself and weather easing off again.

Communication now established with British ship S/S Cairnvalona, and progress continued. Weather fortunately remains fine, and arrived Aberdeen safely.

May 14 (Sat)

8.00pm Arrived ABERDEEN.

Cargo discharged and temporary repairs effected.

End of Voyage.

Signed off May 16th.

Home on leave May 19th - 30th.

Well he wrote all that down cool as a cucumber. But it scared *me*! And *I* knew he would survive it. But, then, he was only 19 at the time so probably thought he was immortal.

Jack signed on S/S "Gyp" again at Aberdeen on June 1st. It seems he wasn't superstitious!

Northern Europe - showing ports visited in Iceland, Finland, Sweden, Norway, Denmark, Germany, Netherlands, Belgium, France and southern Ireland

7. A Peaceful but Slow Burning Time

Maps: Home(Britain):pages 6/7   Northern Europe:page 35
Canada:page 12

S/S Gyp 2 June to 23 July 1921 [about seven weeks]:
from Aberdeen to Rotterdam and back. Then from Aberdeen
to Port Alfred PQ (Province of Quebec, Canada), returning to
Gravesend (River Thames, South-East England).

The leg from Aberdeen to Rotterdam and back (June 2nd
to 9th) was straightforward. The ship then left Aberdeen in
ballast (no cargo) on June 11th, bound for Canada.

June 12 (Sun)	2.00pm Rounding DUNCANSBY HEAD. **Very bad coal and only making about 5 knots.**
June 13 (Mon)	Noon: Off the BUTT OF LEWIS (Hebrides). **Average speed for 12th and 13th only 4.7 knots and for 13th and 14th only 3.2. Moderate head winds and very bad coal - German [!] (Unable obtain coal in UK owing to coal strike.)** Cleaning all six fires each watch and only 60 - 90 lbs [psi] of steam [normally 180]. Speed and weather both improve later. Weather becomes cold and foggy. Sighted slight amount of ice.

Port of Bagotville in Ha Ha Bay, Canada

37

June 30 (Thu)	9.00am Arrived PORT ALFRED PQ (Ha Ha Bay). ... Loaded full cargo of paper pulp (wet - sulphide) and 200 tons bunkers. Five tiers of pulp on deck.
July 8 (Fri)	12.45pm Left PORT ALFRED PQ, bound Gravesend. Anchored in Tadoussac Bay owing to **thick smoke from forest fires rendering navigation dangerous** in Seguenay River. Remained at anchor until 4.30am July 9th.
July 23 (Sat)	9.30pm Arrived GRAVESEND. Signed off July 25th. End of Voyage. Home on leave July 26th - 30th.

A short and fairly uneventful trip, not helped by having to use poor quality coal, which made it slow. It's interesting that UK coal miners were striking as early as 1921 and that, three years after the end of the war, even coal still was frowned upon if it was from Germany.

Jack signed on S/S "Gyp" again, for its next trip:
S/S Gyp   30 July to 7 Sep 1921 [five and a half weeks]: from Gravesend to South Shields, Port Alfred PQ (Canada) and back to Gravesend - a very straightforward trip although, between August 5th and 14th, the log reports "Vessel rolling heavily at times."

Home on leave from September 9th - 15th then back to S/S "Gyp" again:

S/S Gyp   15 Sep to 23 Oct 1921 [five and a half weeks]: from Gravesend to South Shields, Port Alfred PQ and Queenborough (River Medway, South-East England) - a pretty straightforward trip but a couple of problems:

Sept 15 (Thu)	3.30pm Left GRAVESEND, light ship, bound Tyne Dock, South Shields. **Propeller works loose on voyage round.**
Sept 17 (Sat)	9.00am Arrived SOUTH SHIELDS. ... entered Smith's Dry Dock, South Shields, for repairs to propeller. Came out of dock 4.00am Monday, Sept 19th.
Sept 21 (Wed)	5.00pm Left TYNE DOCK, South Shields, in ballast, bound Port Alfred PQ ,Canada.
Sept 22 (Thu)	9.30am Abeam of BUCHAN NESS. **Heavy sea and terrific tide race in Portland Firth and vessel refuses to answer helm.** Put about when two miles south of Duncansby Head and anchored in Sinclair Bay at 9.30pm to await turn of the tide. Up anchor again at 1.30am Sept 23rd.

.....

An unremarkable trip apart from those two incidents.

Jack again signed on to S/S "Gyp" for his last trip on her, which was rather more challenging.

8. A Testing, Icy Trip

Maps: Home(Britain):pages 6/7 Canada:page 12

S/S Gyp 1 Nov to 25 Dec 1921 [eight weeks]:
from Queenborough to Canada - Saguenay River entrance, Quebec, Levis, Quebec, Saguenay River entrance, Quebec - and home to South Shields (River Tyne, North East England).

Nov 3	9.00pm Abeam of BISHOP ROCK (Scilly Isles).
(Thu)	Bad weather right across to Belle Isle. Strong **head winds and heavy sea. Vessel rolling heavily.**
Nov 17	1.30am Abeam of HEATH POINT (Anticosti
(Thu)	Island) ... heavy sea and much snow in the Gulf of St Lawrence. Very cold weather.
Nov 18	7.00pm **Vessel runs aground in dense fog**, in
(Fri)	St Etienne Bay, Saguenay River ... **All efforts to refloat vessel unavailing**, so assistance sent for by W/T. Tug "Chicoutaine" arrived from Ha Ha Bay at 5.30pm Nov 19th. **Efforts at refloating still unavailing. Vessel on shelf with stern overhanging into deep water and bows under high cliffs high and dry on rocks at low water. Bilge keel stripped off on port side. Several large holes in bow and many plates strained. Nos 1 and 2 holds fill and empty with state of tide.** At 10.00am Nov 20th, salvage tug "Lord Strathcona" arrives from Quebec. Holes patched temporarily with cement and kedge anchor put out aft. At 6.00pm (high water), vessel refloated with aid of "Chicoutaine" and "Lord Strathcona" and kedge anchor. Anchored in river. **Vessel making water fast, but salvage pump (put aboard from Lord Strathcona) able to cope with it.** At 3.00am Nov 21st, left St Etienne Bay, proceeding under own steam to Quebec, for dry docking. "Lord Strathcona" standing by to assist if necessary. Arrived Quebec 6.00pm. Anchored.

Not life threatening, but three days of considerable hassle. "W/T" means Wireless Telegraph - radio and morse code - so our Sparks would have been well needed there. And there was more discomfort to come:

Nov 23
(Wed)

11.30am ... Went into Lauzon Dry Dock for repairs to bottom.... Only temporary repairs effected , holes being caulked and cemented, owing to navigation season for St Lawrence being nearly over [i.e it was about to ice up and so would be closed for the winter]. **Nearly all plates in bottom condemned but temporary Lloyds certificate granted conditional on thorough repairs being executed on arrival home, together with thorough repairs to bow (previously damaged by iceberg).** Came out of dry dock Nov 26th (Sat) and **discovered H.P. cylinder cracked by intense cold.** Temporary repairs effected in Quebec.
[H.P. means high pressure - the H.P. cylinder was a major engine part].

.....

Nov 27
(Sun)

5.00pm Left QUEBEC, bound Port Alfred P.Q. 8.00pm **Arrived off entrance to Saguenay River and anchored on account of ice. Proceeded 6.00am Nov 28 and got 20 miles upstream, to St Louis Island, finding Saguenay blocked by ice at that point and impassable. Turned round and re-entered St Lawrence. Put about again at 2.00pm and made another attempt to reach Port Alfred but blocked again at St Louis Island at 4.30pm. Turned round and again re-entered St Lawrence. Proceeded to Bic Island and anchored awaiting orders. Ordered to follow ice breaker "Montcalm" up Saguenay river but these orders cancelled on Nov 30th owing to "Montcalm" being delayed. Now ordered proceed Quebec to load.**

	Left Bic Island anchorage at 4.15pm, Nov 30th, bound Quebec.
	(Very cold weather with heavy snow and much ice in the river. Compelled to anchor at midnight Nov 30th ... as buoys not in position and heavy snow storm in progress. Proceeded
Dec 1	at daylight Dec 1st but **progress very difficult**
(Thu)	**and slow on account of heavy ice in river**).
	5.30pm Arrived QUEBEC.
	...took in 390 tons of bunkers and fresh water. Loaded full cargo of paper pulp ...
Dec 9	7.30am Left QUEBEC, bound Tyne Dock, South
(Fri)	Shields.
	Heavy ice in river for 100 miles below Quebec and much difficulty experienced in getting clear. We are last ship to go down river this season, except Canadian S/S E.R.Crowe, which left six hours after us and stuck in ice 50 miles below Quebec. Do not know if she got clear. Canadian ice-breaker "Montcalm" laid up in Sydney CB. Very cold weather.
Dec 10	Passed FATHER POINT.
(Sat)	River pilot dropped here.
	Much loose ice for some distance down stream, but progress now quite easy.
Dec 12	1.15pm ...**heavy gale** and moderate sea.
(Mon)	
Dec 14	3.00am ... **Thick fog** and heavy weather.
(Wed)	
.....	
Dec 23	4.00pm Off the BUTT OF LEWIS, Hebrides.
(Fri)	Moderate weather across Atlantic.
Dec 25	1.00pm Arrived TYNE DOCK, South Shields.
(Sun)	

No mention of it being Christmas, the day they arrived back.
Just another working day.

Left ship Dec 30th.
Home on leave Dec 30th 1921 to Jan 16th 1922.
Returned to Newcastle.

Appointed to **S/S Spilsby**, Jan 20th 1922. Operator in Charge.

I think he was well shot of S/S Gyp, whose voyages had been rather more adventurous than ideal. By 1930 she had been through the names of "Ballochmyle" and "Kylestrome" - both of which sound Scottish - and had then become "Dimitris", registered in Greece.

A typical radio cabin on a typical ship

9. Round and About in Heavy Weather

Maps: Home(Britain):pages 6/7   Mediterranean:pages 20/21
USA:page 50   Northern Europe:page 35

S/S Spilsby, 22 January to 17 July 1922 [nearly six months]:
Initially to the Mediterranean, then USA via the Caribbean and returning home via Scandinavia.

In more detail: Dunston-on-Tyne to Porto Ferrago (Isle of Elba, Italy), Algiers, Bermuda, Norfolk Va., Nuevitas (Cuba), New York, Baltimore Md. then Scandinavian ports - Aalborg/Norresundby, Odense, Malmo, Kalmar, Jacobstadt, Yxpilla, Himango - and home to West Hartlepool (North East England). Carried coal, sugar, grain, pit props and pulp wood. ...

S/S Spilsby
Built 1910
Gross Registered Tonnage 3673
Length 347 feet
Beam 51 feet
Horse Power 96: Steam driven piston engine, coal fuelled.

Jan 22	Joined ship ... loading 6000 tons of coal.
(Sun)	10.00am Left DUNSTON-ON-TYNE, bound Porto Ferrago, Island of Elba, Italy.
	Swung ship off Tynemouth and adjusted compass ... Thick fog at intervals ...
.....	
Jan 30	12.30pm Abeam of FINISTERRE.
(Mon)	(Very bad weather in Bay of Biscay. Average speed about 4 knots).
.....	
Feb 8	1.00pm Arrived PORTO FERRAGO, Isle of Elba.
(Wed)	**Bad weather outside and unable to get into harbour on account of high wind and heavy sea. Arrived outside harbour 2.00am Feb 7th**

and stood off and on till 9.00am Feb 8th.
Proceeded towards harbour in very cold
weather (snow on hills). Ran aground inside
harbour at 1.00pm Feb 8th. Attempts to
refloat vessel unsuccessful. Further
unsuccessful attempts made at 6.00am and
5.00pm on Feb 9th. Discharged 300 tons of
cargo into lighters and vessel refloated with
aid of tugs and kedge anchor at 7.00pm Feb
10th. ... Berthed at 9.00am Feb 14th and began
discharging with electric cranes, working
intermittently day and night.

.....

Feb 22   7.00pm Arrived ALGIERS. Loaded 150 tons of
(Wed)   bunkers.

.....

Feb 25   3.00pm Passed EUROPA POINT, Gibraltar.
(Sat)   Encountered strong head winds and high
             seas. Making poor progress. Bad weather on
             March 12th and 13th. Vessel hove to about
             1050 miles east of Cape Henry, Va. Hove to
             again for 23 hours on 18th and 19th while
             still 800 miles from Cape Henry, Va. Bunkers
             and fresh water getting low. On Mar 22nd,
             6.00pm, when 250 miles due north of
             Bermuda, discovered insufficient coal
             remaining to reach Newport News, Va.
             Turned south and proceeded towards
             Bermuda. On Mar 23rd at 6.00pm when 70
             miles north of Bermuda, bunkers almost
             empty. Heavy weather and making no
             progress, so engine stopped to save coal.
             Mar 24th, still heavy weather and ship
             drifting rapidly. Wirelessed to Bermuda for
             assistance. Salvage tug "Powerful" arrives at
             midnight Mar 24th, after considerable
             trouble in locating us. Mar 25th, 1.30am,
             tow-lines on board and proceeded towards
             Bermuda in charge of tug.

Mar 25	8.00am Arrived BERMUDA.
(Sat)	... took in 170 tons of bunkers from lighters - also stores and fresh water **(Water and food very low and shifting boards sawn up for fuel.)**
Mar 26	7.30am Left BERMUDA, bound Newport News,
(Sun)	Va. for orders. Fine weather.

In these days of Satnav, radar and satellite communications, it's strange to hear of a salvage tug having "considerable difficulty in locating us" but that was then, not now.

After that bit of excitement all seems to have gone well. The record of the rest of the voyage, which follows, isn't dramatic but gives a feel for how a jobbing cargo ship proceeded. It seemed to take a long time to load and unload and to get access to wharfs etc. Perhaps they had to sit around sometimes waiting for a customer to come up with a job for them.

Mar 31	In Norfolk, Va. took in fuel and fresh water.
(Fri)	Chartered by Munson's of New York.
	Left for Nuevitas, Cuba, with no cargo on board.
Apr 7	11.30am Arrived NUEVITAS, Cuba. Loaded full
(Fri)	cargo (6000 tons) of sugar.
Apr 18	4.00pm Left NUEVITAS, bound New York.
(Tue)	Arrived NEW YORK April 25th. Discharged full cargo, leaving wharf 2.00pm April 28th.
Apr 29	4.45pm Left NEW YORK, bound Baltimore.
(Sat)	
May 1	7.30 pm Arrived BALTIMORE MD.
(Mon)	... May 2nd at Gibson's Wharf, erected grain fittings. May 4th shifted to Baltimore and Ohio R.R's Elevator C and began loading. May 8th, shifted to Pennsylvania R.R. Co's Elevator No 3 and completed loading. Full cargo of grain (rye, oats, wheat and maize). Bunkered from lighters at last two berths.

May 10 (Wed)	4.00pm Left BALTIMORE,MD., bound Aalborg, Denmark.
.....	
May 29 (Mon)	10.00pm Abeam of CAPE WRATH. Thick fog banks. Eased down to wait for tide through Portland Firth. Weather cold but good.
June 2 (Fri)	Arrived AALBORG, Denmark. Discharged 1900 tons of grain with elevators.
June 7 (Wed)	2.00am Left AALBORG, bound Norresundby. 3.00am Arrived Norresundby and took on 350 tons of bunkers, and fresh water. 2.00pm Left NORRESUNDBY, bound Odense, Denmark.
June 8 (Thu)	9.00am Arrived ODENSE and discharged 500 tons of grain with ship's own winches.
.....	
June 11 (Sun)	3.00pm Arrived MALMO, Sweden. ... discharged about 1800 tons of grain ...
June 16 (Fri)	2.30pm Arrived KALMAR, Sweden ... discharged remainder of cargo (about 2000 tons) with elevators and winches.
June 21 (Wed)	Noon. Left KALMAR, light ship, bound Jacobstadt, Finland for orders. [then went to Yxpilla, Finland for Customs clearance and then Himango, Finland.]
June 24 (Sat)	11.30am Arrived HIMANGO. ... Began loading pit props on June 26th at anchor. Props floated off in rafts and booms. Loaded 1300 fathoms of pit-props and 300 fathoms of pulp wood. Eighteen feet of deck cargo. [curious use of units here - a fathom is a length of just over 6 feet, sort of understandable for the total length of many booms of wood, but maybe he meant tons of pulp wood].
July 10 (Mon)	10.00pm Left HIMANGO, bound West Hartlepool.
.....	

July 17   3.00pm Arrived WEST HARTLEPOOL
(Mon)   Began discharging morning of July 18th.
            Left ship July 20th.

Home on leave July 20th to August 13th.
Appointed to **S/S "Levenpool"**, lying at Blyth on Aug 14th.
Operator in Charge.

USA - showing eastern and southern ports - together with Mexico and the Caribbean Sea

10. Going, but not smoothly

Maps: Home(Britain):pages 6/7   USA:page 50
Canada: page 12   Northern Europe:page 35

S/S Levenpool, 15 August to 30 October 1922 [11 weeks]:
To eastern seaboard of USA and Canada and returning home
via Holland with a side trip to southern Ireland to refuel.

In more detail: From Blyth (North East England) to Boston
(USA), Montreal (Canada), Queenstown (now Cobh, Cork
Harbour, Eira), Rotterdam (Holland) and home to Cardiff
(Wales/River Severn). Carried coal, then grain.

S/S Levenpool	
Built 1911	
Gross registered Tonnage 4844	
Length 376 feet	
Beam 57 feet	
Horse Power 442: Steam driven piston engine, coal fuelled.	

Aug 14 (Tue)	Vessel loading full cargo of coal (7600 tons) and 1100 tons bunkers.
Aug 15 (Wed)	8.15pm Left BLYTH for Boston, Mass. U.S.A. Fog on morning of 16th, and cold weather.
Aug 17 (Fri)	1.00am ....Strong adverse tide in Pentland Firth and progress very slow. Strong wind and moderate sea. Heavy rain and cold weather ... Very heavy weather on night of 23rd Aug. **Vessel pitching heavily and shipping heavy water. Progress very slow ... Strong winds and heavy sea till Aug 25th, followed by dense fog at intervals** ... Sep 1st to 5th: Intermittent dense fog ...
Sep 5 (Tue)	3.00pm Arrived BOSTON, MASS. Anchored in harbour awaiting berth. **Harbour congested with coal-laden vessels owing to American coal strike.** Remained at anchor till

	6.00am Sept 17th (Sun). Then alongside at South Boston and discharged. Working day and night with grabs and finished discharging. 7.45am Sep 19th. Moved to anchorage and fumigated.
Sep 19 (Tue)	5.30pm Left BOSTON, light ship.

.....

Sep 25 (Mon)	5.00pm Arrived MONTREAL ... awaiting loading berth ...Thursday Sep 28th... commenced loading grain. Sat, Sep 30th ... lay idle. Sun Oct 1st, moved ... Began loading again Monday morning, Oct 2nd. Finished at 4.30pm. Full cargo of grain. Ready for sea 11.00pm.
Oct 3 (Tue)	5.30am Left MONTREAL, bound Rotterdam. **Thick smoke from forest fires** encountered below Three Rivers. At 8.00pm anchored 20 miles above Quebec, waiting for smoke to lift. At 6.00am, Oct 4th, moved 10 miles further downstream, **but smoke again closed in** and anchor dropped again. Under way again at 4.30pm but **compelled to anchor several times** for brief periods ...

.....

Oct 9 (Mon)	2.30am Abeam of CAPE RACE, Newfoundland. **Dense fog** in vicinity of Cape Race, followed by rain and rough weather. Weather now warmer. **Strong easterly gales from Oct 16th onwards and progress greatly delayed. Running short of coal** and now making for Queenstown [now Cobh, Cork Harbour, southern Ireland] for bunkers. **[and no mention at all, but Jack had his 21st birthday, officially adult, about now].**
Oct 21 (Sat)	9.00am Arrived QUEENSTOWN ... took in 150 tons of bunkers from lighters.
Oct 22 (Sun)	1.00pm Left QUEENSTOWN, bound Rotterdam.

.....

Oct 25	6.00pm Arrived ROTTERDAM.
(Wed)	Discharged full cargo of grain in the Maashaven.
Oct 27	4.00pm Left ROTTERDAM,light ship, bound
(Fri)	Cardiff.
.....	
Oct 29	9.00am Rounding the LIZARD.
(Sun)	**Wind now very strong and sea rough. Anchored in MOUNTS BAY at 9.45am as unable to round Land's End owing to bad weather. Attempted to get round at 6.00am Oct 30th but compelled to put back for shelter as vessel will not steer.** Remained at anchor until 10.00pm then proceeded.
.....	
Oct 31	4.00pm Arrived CARDIFF.
(Tue)	

Home on leave Nov 4th to 8th then rejoined S/S Levenpool, now lying in Swansea, on Nov 9th but left her on Nov 10th. Appointed to **S/S Baron Forbes**, lying at Penarth (Cardiff), Nov 10th. Operator in Charge.

11. Some Rough Times at Sea and Ashore

Maps: Home(Britain):pages 6/7   Mediterranean:pages 20/21

S/S Baron Forbes, 11 November 1922 to 8 January 1923
[eight weeks] to the Mediterranean and back:
From   Cardiff/Penarth   to   Piraeus (Athens port, Greece),
Bizerta (Tunisia), Almeria (Spain), Arzew (Algeria), Huelva
(Spain) and home to Glasgow (west Scotland). Carryied coal,
esparto grass and copper ore.

S/S Baron Forbes
Built 1915 (in Germany)
Gross Registered Tonnage 3061
Length 303 feet
Beam 43 feet
Horse Power 253; Steam driven piston engine, coal fired.

At the time Jack joined, S/S Baron Forbes had just been
bought by H. Hogarth and Sons of Glasgow from Byron Steam
Ship Company. She had formerly been named S/S General
Napier and was an ex-German vessel.

Nov 11	... loading full cargo of coal (approx 4200 tons) ...
(Sat)	10.00pm Left PENARTH, Glamorganshire, bound Piraeus, Greece.
.....	
Nov 22	Abeam of PANTELLARIA ISLAND.
(Wed)	Moderate head wind and sea, retarding progress. Vessel pitching heavily.
	Nov 23rd strong head wind and heavy sea.
.....	
Nov 27	6.00am Arrived PIRAEUS.
(Mon)	Moored stern on in outer harbour and discharged full cargo into lighters. Took in 20 tons of bunkers. Held up 24 hours for boiler water. **Harbour badly congested with relief**

**vessels bringing refugees from Turkish
massacres in Smyrna. All public buildings,
railway stations etc in Piraeus and Athens
commandeered to house refugees. Also
King's Palace and grounds at Athens. Delay
in obtaining boiler water on account of
difficulty experienced in obtaining sufficient
water for enormous numbers of refugees.**

Dec 6 (Wed)	4.00pm Left PIRAEUS, light ship, bound Bizerta, Tunis.
Dec 7 (Thu)	7.30am Strong head winds and rough sea after passing Cape Matapan. Very slow progress.

.....

Dec 11
(Mon)

2.30am Abeam of CAPE BON.
**Very heavy northerly gale springs up now.
Vessel will not answer helm and nearly
blows ashore, but just gets clear after very
hard struggle. Passed Zembra Island at
9.00am but no shelter obtainable so
proceeded. Nearly ashore again on Zembra.
At 3.30pm anchored in sheltered bay behind
Cape Farina. Terrific squalls at times. Both
anchors down and engines going slow ahead.
Remained at anchor till 6.00am Dec 13th
(Wednesday)** when weather eases
considerably. Proceeded towards Bizerta.

Dec 13
(Wed)

Arrived BIZERTA, Tunis.
Alongside and took in 340 tons of bunkers and
boiler water.

Dec 14
(Thu)

9.30 pm Left BIZERTA, bound Algiers for orders.
Ordered by W/T to proceed Almeria, Spain.

.....

Dec 17
(Sun)

5.30pm Arrived ALMERIA.
**Lay stern on to breakwater till 3.00pm Dec
18th owing to King Alfonso being in Almeria
reviewing troops on quayside and no ships
allowed alongside. Then went alongside and
loaded 350 tons of esparto grass. Held up by
bad weather for 30 hours after ready for sea,**

as unable to get out of harbour in heavy cross seas.

Dec 21 (Thu)   6.30am Left ALMERIA, bound Arzew, Algeria ...
8.30pm Arrived ARZEW.
Anchored till daylight. Then alongside and commenced loading esparto grass at 1.30pm Dec 22nd. Loaded 800 tons and finished loading 6.00pm Dec 24th. **Vessel ranging badly in heavy swell. Lines carrying away and difficulty experienced in keeping vessel alongside.** Moved out into bay when cargo finished and anchored till 7.00am Dec 25th.

Dec 25 (Mon)   Left ARZEW, bound HUELVA, Spain.
Fine Weather. [Again, no mention of Christmas. Just another working day.]

.....

Wearing "Whites" – somewhere warm

Dec 27	6.00am Arrived HUELVA, Spain ... loaded
(Wed)	3070 tons of copper ore.
Dec 31	9.00am Left HUELVA, bound Glasgow.
(Sun)	

.....

| Jan 8 | 1.00am Arrived GLASGOW ... discharged full |
| (Mon) | cargo. |

On Jan 9th Jack signed off and took a week's leave.
On Jan 15th he signed on again, same ship, same port.

S/S Baron Forbes, 17 January to 8 March 1923 [7 weeks]:
Glasgow to Troon (just down the Scottish west coast) and
then to the Mediterranean and back home. Specific ports
were Genoa (Italy), Almeria (Spain), Gibraltar, Huelva
(Spain), Lisbon (Portugal), returning to Glasgow.

This was a fairly similar trip to the last one but without the
extreme weather. There were no difficulties this time with a
port's resources being dominated by the needs of refugees.
Cargos as before were coal, esparto grass and copper ore
though, at Lisbon, they loaded some general cargo - mainly
wine, various configurations of cork, and resin.

Apart from "Very heavy weather in the Gulf of Lions" and, in
Huelva, "Finished loading 5.00pm Feb 23rd but held up by
stress of weather until following morning" and "more heavy
weather in Irish Sea" it appears to have been an uneventful
voyage.

Mar 9 (Fri) End of Voyage, at Glasgow, Princes Dock.

Transferred to **S/S "Baron Garioch"** that same day at
request of [same] owners.
Operator in Charge.

S/S "Baron Garioch" was also lying in Princes Dock, loaded
with coal, completing boiler repairs etc, after first survey and
a lay-up of one month.

This photograph is at Almeria, Spain and shows lighters being
used to carry cargo between shore and ship - obviously a slow
and clumsy process compared with modern bulk carriers and
container ships.

12. Long-term, Sea-going Delivery Van

Maps: Home(Britain):pages 6/7   Mediterranean:pages 20/21

S/S Baron Garioch was broadly similar to, but a little smaller than, the previous ships. Jack stayed assigned to this ship for nearly three years. Mostly, the trips were a matter of routine but there were patches of bad weather and a few incidents to add interest which could probably have been done without!

S/S Baron Garioch
Built 1918
Gross Registered Tonnage 2508
Length 303 feet
Beam 43 feet
Horse Power 217: Steam driven piston engine, coal fuelled.

S/S Baron Garioch, 11 March to 19 April 1923
[five and a half weeks]: Glasgow to Genoa, Almeria (both in the Mediterranean), Bilbao (north Spain) and home to Glasgow. An undramatic trip, described here to convey the routine. It went like this:

Left GLASGOW; Abeam of Corshill Point (dirty weather in the Irish Sea); Abeam of Tuskar Rock; Passed the Scillies; Abeam of Finisterre (fine weather); Abeam of the Burlines; Abeam of Cape Roca; Rounding Cape St Vincent; Abeam of Europa Point, Gibraltar (weather fresh); Abeam of Cape de Gata; Abeam of Cape Palos (fine weather); Passing Ivica; Abeam Ile do Levant; **Arrived GENOA** ... Discharged full cargo; Off Porquerolles, Iles d'Hyeres; Abeam of Cape de la Nao; Abeam of Cape Palos; Abeam of Cape de Gata; **Arrived ALMERIA** ... Loaded 700 tons esparto grass; Abeam of Europa Point; Rounding Cape St Vincent (fine weather); Abeam of Cape Roca; Passed the Burlings; Rounding Finisterre; Abeam of Cape Penas; **Arrived BILBAO** ... Loaded 3300 tons iron-ore; Left Bilbao (very heavy weather in the Bay of Biscay); Abeam of Lands End (weather moderating); Abeam of the Tuskar

Rock (10 miles east. Weather freshening again and cold.);
Abeam of Corshill Point; Passed Ailsa Craig; **Arrived
GLASGOW** ... Discharged full cargo (4000 tons) and took in
100 tons bunkers. **End of Voyage.**

Home on leave April 21st - 25th then rejoined in Rothesay
Dock.

S/S Baron Garioch, 27 April to 9 July 1923
[10 and a half weeks]: Clydebank (Scottish west coast) to
Cardiff (Wales) then to Mediterranean ports (Marseilles,
Arzew, Oran) and home to Granton/Edinburgh (Scottish east
coast). Carried coal from Cardiff to Marseilles and esparto
grass from Arzew and Oran to Granton/Edinburgh - they had
difficulty getting this cargo, very little was loaded each day
and they sailed 200 tons light being unable to obtain full
cargo.

Then, continuing, **13 July to 2 September 1923**
[seven weeks]: Granton to South Shields (down Great
Britain's east coast), Marseilles and Toulon (Mediterranean)
and Larne (north east Ireland). Carried coal from South
Shields to Marseilles; and bauxite from Toulon to Larne.

Home on leave September 3rd to 7th.

11 September to 26 October 1923 [six and a half weeks]:
Larne to Ardrossan and Troon (both on the Scottish west
coast) and then to Mediterranean ports (Savona, Garucha,
Carboneras and Almeria) and home to Granton/Edinburgh.
Coal and Esparto Grass again - with one or two interruptions
to routine:

Sep 11 (Tue)	11.30am. Left LARNE, light ship, bound Ardrossan.
	Anchored off Ardrossan at 6.30pm in half gale, waiting for tide.
	10.30pm entered dry-dock. Vessel's bottom cleaned and painted.

Sep 13 (Thu)	1.30pm Left ARDROSSAN, light ship, bound Troon. 3.30 pm Arrived TROON ... loaded full cargo of coal and bunkers. Total about 4200 tons. Also took in 200 tarpaulins for grass cargo.
Sep 18 (Tue)	6.45pm Left TROON, bound Savona, Italy. Anchored outside till 9.15pm waiting for sailor, to complete complement.
.....	[ten days to get from west Scotland to Italy!]
Sep 28 (Fri)	10.45pm Arrived SAVONA ... discharged full cargo.
Oct 5 (Fri)	7.00pm Left SAVONA, bound Garrucha, Spain.
.....	
Oct 8 (Mon)	11.15am Arrived GARRUCHA, Spain ... loaded 200 tons esparto grass from lighters. Discharged 60 tarpaulins.
Oct 9 (Tue)	12.15pm Left GARRUCHA, bound Carboneras. Lighters in tow. 2.00 pm Arrived CARBONERAS. Anchored and loaded 800 tons esparto grass from lighters ...
Oct 12 (Fri)	7.45pm Left CARBONERAS, bound Almeria. Towed lighters back from Carboneras to Garrucha before proceeding on voyage.
Oct 13 (Sat)	6.00am Arrived ALMERIA ... completed loading with 1000 tons esparto grass. Six tiers on deck.
Oct 18 (Thu)	1.30pm Left ALMERIA, bound Granton/Edinburgh.
.....	
Oct 26 (Fri)	3.00am Arrived GRANTON. Alongside and discharged full cargo. End of Voyage.

Home on leave just over a week, from Oct 27th - Nov 5th and rejoined the ship in Grangemouth (River Forth, so same vicinity), Nov 6th.

Commenced loading noon Nov 7th. Loaded full cargo and bunkers. Total 4150 tons. Finished loading 2.00pm Nov 8th.

6 November to 17 December 1923 [six weeks]: River Forth (Edinburgh and Grangemouth) to Italy (Naples) and Spain (Valencia, Gandia and Cartegana) then home to London. Some bad weather and other incidents:

.....

Nov 20	2.00am Arrived NAPLES.
(Tue)	Anchored till 3.00pm for weather to moderate. Then stern on to wharf ... Began discharging into lighters 8.30am Nov 21st. **No work on 23rd owing to bad weather and heavy rain. Heavy gale on Friday night, Nov 23rd. Many ships adrift and schooners and lighters sunk and damaged.** Discharged full cargo.
Nov 27	3.45pm Left NAPLES, light ship, bound Valencia,
(Tue)	Spain ...

This photograph is at Savona, Italy. The ship is probably S/S Baron Garioch - the name on the stern is not fully clear but it seems to match, and the context points to this ship.

Dec 1	1.30pm Arrived VALENCIA. Entered harbour.
(Sat)	8.30am Dec 2nd. No work on 2nd or 3rd.
	Fumigated on 3rd. Then loaded part cargo
	(oranges, onions, nuts, tinned fruit, etc).
	Finished loading 1.00am Dec 6th.
Dec 6	2.00am Left VALENCIA, bound Gandia, Spain.
(Thu)	6.50am Arrived GANDIA. Anchored outside in
	moderate gale awaiting berth. Alongside ... and
	commenced loading (fruit) 2.00am Dec 7th.
	Finished loading 10.00pm and Left GANDIA,
	bound Cartegana, Spain.
Dec 8	11.00am Arrived CARTEGANA. Alongside and
(Sat)	completed loading full cargo of fruit etc.
Dec 9	4.00am Left CARTEGANA, bound London.
(Sun)	
.....	
Dec 17	9.00pm Arrived London ... unable to get
(Mon)	alongside till 9.00pm owing to state of tide ...
	discharged full cargo. End of voyage.

The next voyage continued on without a leave break and without leaving the ship.

21 December 1923 to 15 February 1924 [eight weeks]:
London to Troon (west Scotland), then to Mediterranean ports - Genoa (Italy), Valencia & Burriana (Spain) - and returning home via Hamburg (Germany) to Burntisland (River Forth, east Scotland).
Map of Northern Europe:Page 35

Carried coal from Troon to Genoa, general cargo (fruit, wine, rice, resin, onions etc) from Valencia and Burrunia to Hamburg. It was winter and they had some bad weather.

On leaving Troon they had to anchor outside and wait for part of the crew to join. There was very dirty weather in Genoa and heavy weather in the Gulf of Lions. When the ship left Valencia, bound for nearby Burriana, Spain, there was **"Fog on coast and difficulty experienced in locating Burriana."**

Off Dover there was **"Dense fog in North Sea"**. **"Heavy sludge ice in river** [Elbe, on the way to Hamburg] impedes progress."

On arrival at Burntisland at the voyage end, on 15th February, the ship was empty and they immediately started loading a full cargo of coal and full bunkers. A dock strike was due to start the next day but Burntisland was not as yet affected. Loading finished mid-Feb 19th and they went straight on to the next voyage, without a break and without leaving the ship.

19 February to 21 March 1924 [just over four weeks]: Burntisland (east Scotland) to Genoa (Italy), Huelva (Spain) and Glasgow (west Scotland).

The coal cargo was carried to Genoa. They travelled light to Huelva and loaded a full cargo of copper ore to deliver to Glasgow. The voyage seems to have been uneventful apart from nearly being caught in a dock strike and "Strong easterly winds in Bay of Biscay. Ship rolling heavily and shipping heavy water."

The voyage ended on March 21st at Glasgow, where the cargo was discharged and full bunkers were taken on. On 29th March, the ship relocated to Troon, Ayrshire, a little further down the Scottish west coast.

Jack was home on leave from March 24th to March 31st and rejoined the ship at Troon.

Their cargo was delayed on the railway and loading was very slow. But a full cargo of coal was loaded.

31 March to 17 May 1924: A **six-week** round trip to the Mediterranean.
Troon to Savona (Italy); Bone (Algeria) and home to Clydebank. Carried coal from Troon to Savona and iron ore from Bone to Clydebank/Glasgow.

There was heavy weather in the Bay of Biscay and the other bit of excitement happened three days before arriving in Savona: An Italian stowaway was transferred to the ship from S/S Mombasa at midnight April 18th (Good Friday). Mombasa was bound for U.S.A. and the stowaway was taken back to Savona on S/S Baron Garioch to avoid trouble with the U.S. immigration authorities. The transfer was made in Mombasa's dinghy in fine weather.

On arrival in Glasgow the ship discharged its full cargo and loaded a full cargo of coal, and full bunkers.

Home on leave May 19th to 23rd and rejoined the ship in Glasgow.

24 May to 10 July 1924 [eight weeks]: Glasgow (east Scotland) to Italy (Genoa) then Spain (Alicante and Aguilas) and home to the River Forth in west Scotland - Edinburgh/Granton and Tayport.

Carried coal and esparto grass on a routine voyage. At Tayport on July 10th, all remaining cargo was discharged and the ship underwent a survey of the hull, tanks, etc.

On July 18th, the ship travelled empty down the coast to South Shields where it loaded a cargo of coal.

18 July to 3 September 1924 [nearly seven weeks]: Tayport to South Shields then the Mediterranean - Leghorn (Livorno, Italy) and Toulon (south coast of France) and Larne (north east Ireland).

Started, in South Shields, with a full cargo of coal and later carried bauxite. All was routine though there were strong winds and slow progress on 26 July (off the Casquets). But after passing Gibraltar there was a bit of drama:

Aug 1 (Fri)	11.00am **SOS received from Oran FUK advising seaplane in distress, approx. position 100 kilos from Alicante, en route Alicante to Oran. Seaplane left at 14.50 and last heard of at 15.30. Ship about 20 miles**

> from this position. Course altered
> accordingly and on reaching given position
> turned south for 15 miles along track of
> seaplane. Nothing sighted and voyage
> continued at midnight. Other vessels also
> searching, but nothing sighted.

The remainder of the voyage was, again, routine but there was a heavy thunderstorm at Leghorn/Livorno, when leaving, with strong head winds and slow progress. And on August 25th, when abeam of Cape San Antonio, there was a heavy swell with the vessel rolling heavily. There was also thick fog through the night of 29th-30th August. The ship arrived in Larne on September 3rd and discharged its cargo.

Home on leave September 4th to 10th and rejoined the ship at Larne on 11th. [Getting to and from home would have been less straightforward than usual, involving ferries across the Irish Sea as well as railways].

12 September to 8 November 1924 [eight weeks]: Larne to Troon [a short, relocation trip across the Irish Sea from the east coast of Ireland to the west coast of Scotland] then, after loading, on to the Mediterranean (Savona in Italy and Arzew in Algeria) and returning home to the River Forth on the east coast of Scotland (Granton/Edinburgh and Tayport).

Carried coal to Savona and Esparto Grass (six tiers on deck) from Arzew to Granton and Tayport.

A bit of a slow start:

Sep 12	11.15am Left LARNE, light ship, bound Troon.
(Fri)	6.15pm Arrived TROON.
	Entered dry dock on 13th and came out on afternoon of 15th, in heavy gale, and moored alongside west wall. Alongside coal berth on 16th and loaded full cargo of coal. Loading delayed by local holidays (Ayr Races) and by difficulty in obtaining cargo. Weather wild and wet.

It was a straightforward trip after that, apart from a bit of fog and occasional strong winds. Brief spell of leave (8th to 13th November) then rejoined the ship, still at Tayport on 14th.

14 November to 30 December 1924
[nearly seven weeks]: Tayport to Grangemouth (still in the River Forth) then Genoa (Italy) and Seville (Spain) returning to the other side of Scotland at Troon.   Carried coal from Grangemouth to Genoa and Iron Ore from Seville to Troon. A bit of difficulty leaving Seville:

Dec 23 (Tue)	12.45pm Left SEVILLE bound Troon [with full cargo of Iron Ore]. **Aground on river** from 5.00pm to 9.00pm owing to shallow water and low tide. Crossed bar of R. Guadalquivir [Seville's river] 12.30am 24th. Pilot dropped 12.50am.

Heavy weather all the way up the Portuguese coast. On arrival at Troon, had to cruise off and on from 10.30am until 1.00pm owing to bad weather and low tide. Short leave from 3rd to 7th January 1925.

There's a pattern with this ship's voyages. Its foreign ports are mainly in the Mediterranean, or conveniently on the way there or back, and it alternated between the west coast Glasgow area and the east coast Edinburgh area for its Scottish "home" port. The next trip branched out from that routine by heading from the Mediterranean to Iceland rather than directly home (though they did call in to their home area, on the Scottish west coast, to refuel).

Map of Northern Europe:page 35
9 January to 3 March 1925 [seven and a half weeks]:
Troon to Mediterranean - Savona in Italy and Ivica (better known as the island of Ibiza, Spain) - then to Havnefjord in Iceland (via Ayr, Scotland, to take on bunkers) and back to Troon.

Carried coal from Troon to Savona and salt from Ivica to Havnefjord. (No cargo between Savona and Ivica or from Havnefjord to Troon). A straightforward trip apart from some patches of heavy weather. There was no break for leave before the next voyage, which was very similar (Genoa instead of Savona in Italy and Reykjavik instead of Havnefjord in Iceland).

Then, continuing without leaving the ship:

6 March to 5 May 1925 [two months]: Troon to Genoa, Ivica, Ayr (west coast of Scotland, to refuel), Reykjavik (Iceland) and home to the west coast of Scotland (Ardrossan and Clydebank).

Carried coal from Troon to Genoa and salt from Ivica to Reykjavik. Otherwise light ship.

(Very heavy easterly gale along the southern coast of Portugal and Spain in mid-March, with progress very slow. Similarly, between Ayr and Reykjavik in mid-April there was **heavy weather throughout the passage and the vessel hove to in terrific seas on 15th and 19th.**) At the end of the voyage, the ship was directed to go to Ardrossan on May 1st where it was dry docked for fitting a bronze propeller and painting the ship.

On leave from May 2nd to 5th then rejoined the ship at Clydebank. This saw a sudden change from the Mediterranean routine, with a trip to Canada and back.

Map of Canada:page 12
9 May to 18 June 1925 [nearly six weeks]: Clydebank to Montreal and returning to Sharpness (River Severn on the west coast of England - so a different home port).

Carried coal from Clydebank to Montreal and Wheat from Montreal to Sharpness. They took a southerly course across the Atlantic to avoid ice and "Saw three bergs only, May 19th". There was a strong adverse current in the river heading up to Montreal and they had to stop for a couple of hours after leaving Montreal because of fog. But it was essentially a straightforward trip with no hitches.

After three days leave (which he took in Liverpool), Jack rejoined the ship at Sharpness.

Maps: USA:page 50 Cuba:page 72
22 June 1925 to 6 January 1926 [six and a half months]:
A longer and more complex trip, to USA and Cuba, the last voyage on this ship:
Sharpness to Barry (still in the River Severn), Fowey (south coast of England in Cornwall) then to the east coast of USA (Portland Me and Philadelphia Pa), on to north coast Cuba - Havana, Sagua La Grande and Pastellilo (Nuevitas) - then a side trip to southern USA (New Orleans and Mobile) and back to south coast Cuba - Cienfuegos, Santa Cruz del Sur, Guayabal, Manzanillo, Santiago de Cuba, Caimanera, Boqueron and Casilda - then New York/Edgewater NJ followed by the north coast of Cuba again - Pastellilo (Nuevitas), Manati, Chaparra, Jibara,Tarafa (Nuevitas) - then to the east coast of USA again (Baltimore Md and Newport News Va) before returning home to Manchester (inland from the River Mersey, along the ship canal).

They took China Clay from Fowey to Portland; coal from Philadelphia to Havana; sugar from Sagua La Grande and Pastellilo to New Orleans; general cargo from New Orleans and Mobile (together with timber on the deck) to Cienfuegos, Guayabal, Manzanillo, Santiago de Cuba and Caimanera (in Guantanamo Bay). There were holidays on Saturday, Sunday, Monday and Wednesday so this final discharging of cargo at

71

Caimanera took a week. They then moved to Boqueron (also in Guantanamo Bay). From there and Casilda they took sugar to New York, where they bunkered and loaded 1500 tons of general cargo. There was bad weather on the way to Pastellilo, making progress poor.

Ports Visited in Cuba
(USA map on page 50 locates Cuba itself)

They discharged their cargo successively in Pastellilo, Manati, Chaparra and, finally, Jibara. They carried sugar from Puerto Tarafa (Nuevitas) to Baltimore. In Baltimore they loaded a full cargo of grain then travelled overnight to Newport News to take on bunkers and head for home.

But then this generally straightforward voyage of jobbing transport was jolted out of its routine:

| Dec 19 | 10.00pm Left NEWPORT NEWS, bound Lands |
| (Sat) | End for orders. |

Steering to cross longitude 40 West in latitude 40 North. **Encountered terrific westerly gale on Dec 23rd. Extensive damage about decks. Ice-box washed overboard and port saloon alleyway door stove in. Pantry store room and accommodation washed out and stores ruined. Dinghy carried away on port side of lower bridge etc. Running before gale at half speed on a South East course.** Weather abates during 24th **but increases again same night. Starboard saloon alleyway door stove in on 24th and starboard side of lower bridge smashed. Shipping water on top bridge and vessel in danger of foundering.** Weather eases again on 28th and remains moderate to bad for remainder of passage. W/T orders received to proceed Manchester.

1926

Jan 5	8.00pm Arrived in Mersey and anchored off
(Tue)	Liverpool overnight.
Jan 6	2.30pm Arrived MANCHESTER [presumably via
(Wed)	the Ship Canal].
	Berthed at Salford Docks.

This rather dramatic voyage end has another uncharacteristic twist:

Signed off Baron Garioch at Manchester, Jan 7th. **Called out on strike.**

Reported Liverpool Jan 8th and **dismissed Jan 9th.** Home Jan 9th - April 21st, 1926 **[three and a half months].**

Reported at Glasgow April 21st (Wed) for re-instatement in Company.

That was a very long break, presumably unpaid since he had been dismissed as a striker before being re-instated.

Appointed to **RMS S/S Clydesdale** (David MacBrayne Ltd - Glasgow's West Highland Mail S.S. Co) lying in Lamonts Dry Dock, Greenock. Joined ship same day.

Royal Mail Ship: S/S Clydesdale

13. Scottish Interlude

Map of Scotland RMS Clydesdale service:page 76

**RMS Clydesdale, 26 May to 17 August 1926
[nearly three months]:**

RMS Clydesdale Built 1905 Gross Registered Tonnage 401 Length 151 feet Beam 26 feet Horse Power 85: Steam driven piston engine. Coal fueled.

As a Royal Mail Ship, S/S Clydesdale travelled around the Scottish West Coast and Islands, collecting and delivering mail. If it hadn't been a mail run it would have been described as a milk run - continuously hopping from one landing to the next. As well as mail, she also carried passengers and general cargo, including coal, and made a special trip carrying cattle. The time on this ship, with many stopping places, appears to have been uneventful on the whole apart from the occasional note of "bad weather" or "mod. rough passage". There was a minor hitch at the start:

Apr 26   3.25pm Left Greenock bound Kyle of Lochalsh ...
(Mon)   Put back into Greenock 5.25pm with defects on
          deck. Same repaired. Left Greenock again
          8.00pm ...

On 7th May there is a note that they were following an Emergency Timetable owing to a coal strike and RMS Cygnet (presumably a sister ship on the same run) being laid up in consequence.

On 11th May there was a delay leaving Tarbert, due to engine trouble.

LANDING PLACES AND PORTS
Islands, Other Features

STORNOWAY

Lewis

Stockinish

TARBERT
Harris
RODEL
LOCH MADDY

North Uist
DUNVEGAN *(Skye)*
Skye
PORTREE

KYLE OF LOCHALSH
Sound of Sleat
MALLAIG

South Uist
Barra
CASTLEBAY
Rhum
Eigg
LOCH BOISDALE
Canna
Coll
Tiree
KILCHOAN
OBAN
TOBERMORAY

Mull
GLASGOW
Islay
Jura
River Clyde
BOWLING
GREENOCK
RENFREW
Scotland
England

Scotland: West Coast and Islands RMS Clydesdale service

There were many landing places, most too small to call ports. I like the West Coast of Scotland, though my visits to the islands have been limited to Skye and Mull. So I rather enjoyed reading: ... Kyle of Lochalsh [on the mainland, now connected to the Island of Skye with a bridge] ... Tarbert (south Harris Island), Stockinish Island, Rodel (south Harris Island), Loch Maddy (North Uist Island), Loch Boisdale (South Uist Island), Island of Canna, the islands of Rhum and Eigg, Mallaig (on the mainland) and heading up the Sound of Sleat between Skye and the mainland via Armadale (on Skye) and Glenelg (on the mainland) to Kyle of Lochalsh again.

All repeated over and over. The names are music! But maybe they paled after about twelve weeks' repetition. At least it was mainly summer.

Sometimes there were variations: North Uist to South Uist via Dunvegan on Skye, well to the east; or leaving South Uist for Castlebay (Island of Barra), then via the islands of Tiree and Coll to Kilchoan on the mainland and then south to Tobermoray (on the Island of Mull).

Towards the end of Jack's time on this ship it also occasionally went to Stornoway on the Island of Lewis, to the north. And it would head from Tobermoray on Mull to Oban on the mainland then south to calling points on Islay, and sometimes Jura, and across to the River Clyde and Glasgow.

Left RMS Clydesdale on 14th August 1926. Home on leave, for two and a half weeks, until 1st September.

Appointed to **S/S Dunrobin** on September 3rd. Returned home September 4th to 6th and began the voyage, from Glasgow, at noon on September 7th.

14. The Opposite of an Interlude

Maps: Home(Britain):pages 6/7 USA-Mexico:page 50
Cuba:page 72 South America:page 81
Mediterranean:page 20

S/S Dunrobin headed for America and spent over two and a half years as a carrier for hire around North America, South America and the Caribbean. Nowadays, sailors are flown to and fro to join and leave ships, wherever they are, and to have spells of home leave. Not so in the 1920s.

S/S Dunrobin
Built 1924
Gross Registered Tonnage 5041
Length 405 feet
Beam 53 feet
Horse Power 410: Steam driven piston engine, coal fired.

S/S Dunrobin 7 September 1926 - 24 April 1929:
This was a long time away from home so best summarised in sections.

<u>7 Sept 1926 - 1 January 1927 [nearly four months]</u>
Maps: Home:pages 6/7 USA:page 50 South America:page 81

Glasgow, (**bad weather across the Atlantic),** Brooklyn (New York) and Newport News, to Brazilian Ports - Bahia, Victoria, Santos, Rio Grande do Sul, Sao Francisco do Sul, Paranagua, Ceara, Para (**"Vessel on bottom and some time lost in consequence")** and back to Brooklyn. Carried coal and general cargo from Brooklyn and Newport News to Bahia, Victoria, Santos, Rio Grande do Sul, Sao Francisco do Sul and finally Paranagua. Then carried general cargo (hides, wax, rubber, nuts etc) from Ceara and Para to Brooklyn.

At Brooklyn loaded full cargo (case-oil, flour, motor-cars etc) working day and night including New Years Day.

2 Jan 1927 - 3 April 1927 [three months]
Maps: USA:page 50   South America:page 81 (opposite)

With Brooklyn, New York, as a base made a couple of round tips to Brazilian ports:
Brooklyn, Norfolk News, Bahia, Victoria, Rio de Janeiro, Santos, Rio Grande do Sul, Sao Francisco do Sul, Paranagua, Ceara, Para, Brooklyn.   Took general cargo from Brooklyn, bunkered at Newport News, then offloaded cargo at all ports to Paranagua. Picked up some cargo at Rio Grande do Sul, Ceara and Para and took it to Brooklyn.

At Para the ship was again "fast on bottom" and took half an hour to free. **Then "guide rod in engine room ran hot and vessel proceeding dead slow ahead in consequence".** On 18th March, **"stopped in afternoon for 90 mins with engine trouble. Heavy swell and moderate wind. Vessel rolling heavily".** On 24th March **"Terrific gale, with torrential rain in the evening, and very high seas".**

4 April - 6 July 1927 [three months]

A similar round trip to Brazilian ports:
Brooklyn, Norfolk, Bahia, Victoria, Rio di Janeiro, Rio Grande do Sul, Sao Francisco do Sul, Paranagua, Para, Brooklyn.

Loaded general cargo at Brooklyn, bunkered at Newport and discharged cargo at the following ports with final discharge at Paranagua. At Para loaded about 500 tons of Brazil nuts, wax, hides, rubber and general cargo, and took it to Brooklyn.

When anchored inside the harbour at Victoria, **"wire fouled propellor when leaving anchorage - removed by divers"**. Arrival at Rio di Janeiro was delayed by bad weather.

South America - ports visited in Brazil and Chile and the Panama Canal region

<u>7 July - 28 October 1927 [three and a half months]</u>
Maps: USA-Mexico:page 50   Cuba: page 72

With Brooklyn, New York as a base, made trips to Cuba, Mexico and southern USA ports:
Brooklyn, Havana, Matanzas, Caibarien, Sagua La Grande, Cardenas, Sagua La Grande, Caibarien, Galveston, New Orleans, Havana, Progreso, Yalton Ranch Mexico, Campeachy, Baltimore, Plymouth, Norfolk, Matanzas, Brooklyn.

Took general cargo from Brooklyn to Cuba - Havana and ports to Cardenas. Loaded sugar at Sagua La Grande and Caibarien (6000tons/40000bags in all) and discharged it at Galveston (southern USA). Took general cargo (about 300 tons) from New Orleans (USA) to Havana (Cuba). Carried sisal from Progreso (Mexico) to Baltimore (USA) and, within that larger leg, carried dye-wood from Yalton Ranch (Mexico) to Baltimore. Finally, loaded 55000 bags of sugar at Matanzas, Cuba (took 9 working days to load but still 2500 bags short) and discharged it at Brooklyn, USA - at the Pearl Street Sugar Refinery, under Manhattan Bridge.

Yalton Ranch, Mexico was obviously not on the beaten track: **"Yalton not on any available charts. Bonfires lit ashore as landmarks. Shifted out in afternoon as vessel aground".** Loaded part cargo (about 400tons) of dye-wood from lighters.
From 18th to 21st October: considerably delayed by a strong northerly gale since leaving Matanzas.

<u>29 Oct 1927</u> Fumigated.   Moved anchorage and awaiting orders.

<u>16 - 18 Nov 1927</u>. Dry docked. Bottom painted and minor repairs done.

<u>20 Nov 1927 - 29 Jan 1928 [10 weeks]</u>
Maps: USA:page 50   South America:page 81

New York (Brooklyn) - travelled light to - Baltimore (loaded part cargo of sheet iron, bath tubs, wire etc), Norfolk (loaded part cargo of timber and coal, and bunkers), Philadelphia (loaded 100 tons of cement and oil), New York (loaded part cargo of cars, flour, tyres, baths etc) to several ports in Brazil and Argentina.

22 Dec: Arrived Santos (Brazil). Discharged 700 tons bunkers into S/S Commercial Pilot; discharged part general cargo; loaded 500 bags coffee (working Christmas Day), then to Montevideo (strong head winds and moderate seas delay ship), Buenos Airies, Rosario, San Nicolas, Santos ...
    Cargo was discharged at Montevideo, Buenos Aries and finally Rosario. At Rosario about 1300 tons of linseed was loaded, followed by another 5000 tons at San Nicolas.

There's a gap in the records here, seemingly because a notebook is missing.

<u>12 Oct 1928</u> **"Half gale, moderate seas and vessel rolling heavily".**

<u>14 Oct 1928 - 27 Feb 1929 [four and a half months]</u>
Maps: South America:page 81   USA-Mexico:page 50

From Buenos Airies, Argentina, headed south (**"strong winds, heavy sea, vessel rolling heavily"**) and passed east to west through the Straits of Magellan, then northwards to Chile ports **("Very cold weather. Heavy squalls of wind and hail. Dirty night. Strong head wind and increasing sea and [next day] strong beam wind and heavy sea. Vessel rolling heavily")**.
    Called at Iquique, Coleta Buena, Pisagua – then to Balboa (south end of Panama Canal) and through the canal to Colon

at its north end. Then passed through the Yukatan Channel, between Mexico and Cuba ("**strong winds, shipping moderate water and pitching heavily**") to Galveston (berth at foot of Columbus Statue) and Norfolk ("**heavy weather en route, vessel pounding heavily and doing very little**"), Colon again, then Tocopilla (in Chile), Balboa, Panama Canal, Colon, Norfolk, Baltimore, New York/Brooklyn.

While initially empty, they picked up cargo at Iquique, Coleta Buena and Pisagua (and stores and bunkers at Colon) and took it to Galveston. Then they went to Norfolk to be fumigated (on Christmas Day) and travelled empty to Tocopilla to load a full cargo of nitrate in bags (8350 tons) for Norfolk, Baltimore and, finally, New York.

The end of this segment brought rough weather and some delay:

20 Feb 1929 (en route to New York). Strong NE winds and rough sea. Vessel rolling very heavily. Heavy snow and blizzards. Freezing hard.

22-27 Feb 1929 Arrived Brooklyn. Washington's birthday so no work done that day. Discharged remaining (3000 tons of) cargo. Off charter.

They had trouble with the Panama canal because half of it was closed for maintenance:

5 Jan Arrived Colon for canal transit. Delayed 2 hours at Pedromiguel [in the southern section of the Panama Canal] due to repairs to the canal and only one side working.

3 - 4 Feb Arrived Colon via Balboa. (ships going through canal in darkness as well as daylight owing to congestion and delay at Gatua Locks, under repair)

In the middle of this on 13th Jan:
 "Stowaway transferred to us from American S/S Chiloil for return to Tocopilla"

27 Feb - 24 April 1929 [eight weeks]
Maps: USA:page 50   Cuba:page 72   Mediterranean:page 20
Home (Britain):pages 6/7

The ship returned to England, carrying sugar from Cuba to Marseilles (south of France), with some difficulties:

28 Feb Arrived Norfolk. Took on fresh water and about 900 tons bunkers.

1 Mar Left Norfolk, light ship, bound Pal Alto, Cuba.

8 - 14 Mar Arrived Pal Alto and loaded full cargo (8300 tons) of sugar from lighters.

5 April Arrived Gibraltar and took 500 tons bunkers.

9 - 13 April Arrived Marseilles and discharged full cargo with cranes.

20 April 1929 (en route to Falmouth, England) - **"Strong easterly gale springs up pm. Vessel driven far to westward and rolling violently. Engines stopped 10.00am 21st. Strong gale and high seas. Short of coal. Started again 7.45pm. Endeavouring to make Brest [France] for bunkers. Strong headwind and moderate head sea ... Now about 200 miles from Brest and less than 60 tons of coal. Weather moderating gradually and now making for Bishop Rock. Started burning wood on morning of 22nd. Coal very low. Now proceeding Falmouth for bunkers".**

23 April 1929 Arrived Falmouth and took in 50 tons bunkers.

24 April 1929 Arrived Barry Roads (River Severn) and proceeded to Barry Graving Dock.

End of Voyage. Home on (prolonged voyage) leave 26th April until 15th July.

Transferred to Glasgow and went there. Home again on 17th-19th July. In Glasgow over the weekend, 20th-21st July, and appointed to **S/S Clan MacNair**, Monday 22nd July.

15. Floating Scotsmen

Maps: Home (Britain):pages 6/7   Africa:page 88
India:page 89   Middle East:page 25
Northern Europe:page 35

It's a fair bet that the Clan Line, whose ship names started with "Clan" and which used Glasgow as a base, had Scottish connections. Jack sailed on four Clan line ships over time, two of them in this segment of his time at sea.

All these Clan line ships were a notch further along in their technology. In addition to their triple expansion piston engines they had a turbine, taking steam from the exhaust of the low pressure cylinder and extracting further energy from it. This gave more power and greater fuel efficiency. The first Clan Line ship which Jack joined, S/S Clan MacNair, had only just been fitted with its steam turbine. Speed trials with the newly augmented power system were first on the agenda.

In addition, these ships were equipped to fire their boilers with either oil or coal and, of course, they were fitted with fuel tanks for oil as well as retaining their coal bunkers. So they could pick either oil or coal as a fuel depending on cost and availability - that gave them some flexibility and opportunities to pay less for fuel, a handy thing when trying to increase profits.

The territory they serviced was largely new to Jack, too, calling at ports in Africa and India.

S/S Clan MacNair
Built 1921
Gross Registered Tonnage 6096
Length 411 feet
Beam 53 feet
Horse Power 639: Steam driven piston engine with low pressure turbine. Fitted for oil firing, as well as coal.
The turbine was newly fitted in mid-1929.

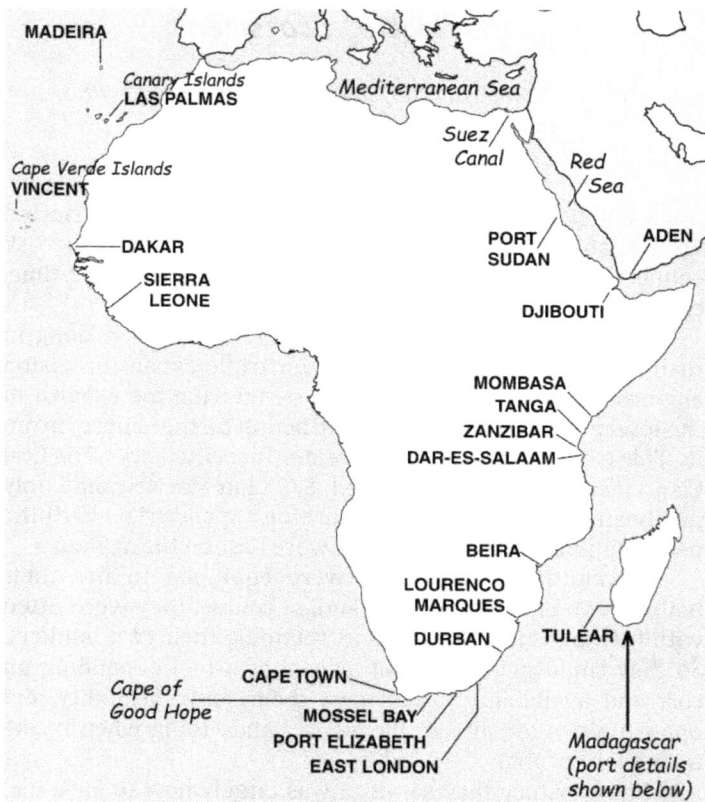

MADEIRA

Canary Islands
LAS PALMAS

Mediterranean Sea

Suez
Canal

Red
Sea

Cape Verde Islands
VINCENT

PORT
SUDAN

ADEN

DAKAR

SIERRA
LEONE

DJIBOUTI

MOMBASA
TANGA
ZANZIBAR
DAR-ES-SALAAM

BEIRA
LOURENCO
MARQUES
DURBAN

TULEAR

Cape of
Good Hope

CAPE TOWN

MOSSEL BAY
PORT ELIZABETH
EAST LONDON

Madagascar
(port details
shown below)

AMBALAHONKO
MAGUNGA
SOARANA
NAMANGOA
LOVOBE)
MORANDARA)
MOROMBE

PORT LOUIS
Mauritius

TULEAR

Reunion

**Africa – Ports visited on the West, East and South coasts,
including Madagascar and offshore islands**

88

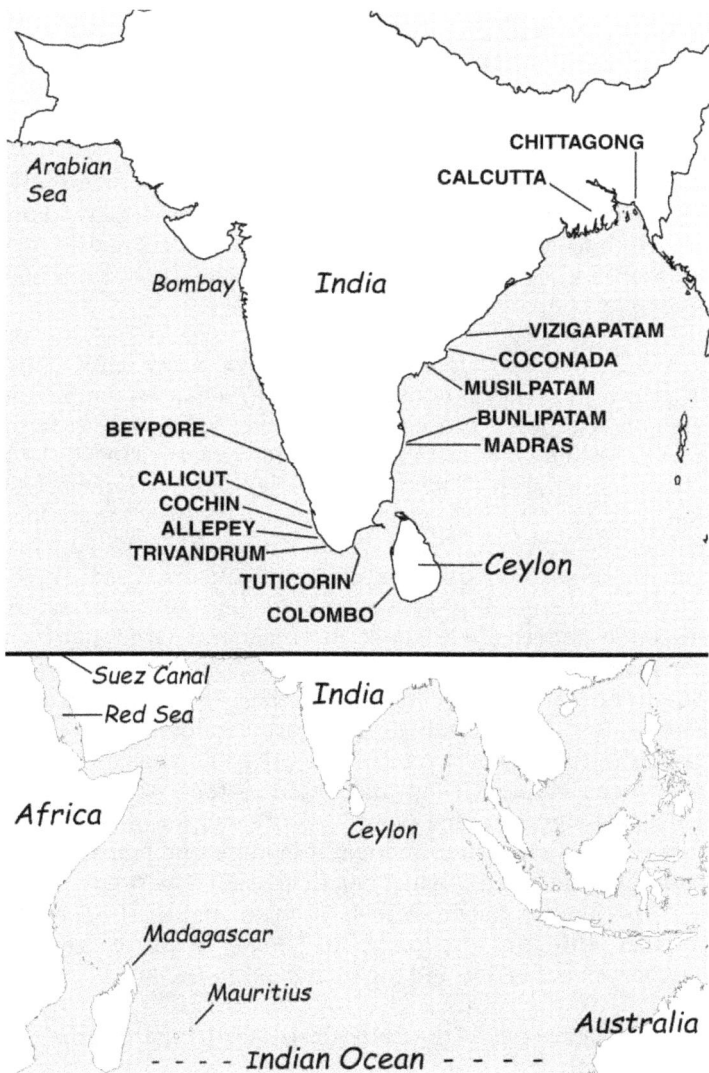

India (and Ceylon) - Ports visited - and the Indian Ocean

S/S Clan MacNair 23 July - 30 Dec 1929

[over five months]: After some local movement in UK went to southern Africa then across to India, returning via the Suez Canal:

Glasgow, Greenock, Newport Mon, Greenock, Glasgow, Birkenhead, then Africa - Cape Town, Mossel Bay, Port Elizabeth (Algoa Bay), East London, Lourenco Marques – followed by India – Chittagong, Madras and Tuticorin – and returning home to Newport Mon and Glasgow.

S/S Clan MacNair had been alongside a dry dock. First action was to take on bunkers, then they adjusted compasses and, on 25th July, "proceeded on speed trials in the Firth of Clyde, testing new auxilliary turbine. Average Speed 14.1 knots [26 km/hr]." Then they travelled light to Newport to load 2500 tons of general cargo (railway materials, galvanised iron etc). On return to Glasgow, they added more general cargo and took on 1800 tons of bunkers.

At Birkenhead they swung the ship to calibrate its direction finders (DF), loaded more general cargo and took on another 100 tons of bunkers. The cargo was all taken to South Africa and successively discharged at Cape Town, Mossel Bay, Port Elizabeth and East London. Apart from taking 13 cars to Lourenco Marques, the ship appears then to have been empty. They took in 1150 tons of bunkers at Lourenco Marques then went to Chittagong in India to load jute. Loaded more jute, and tea, at Madras, and more tea and general cargo, at Tuticorin. Then they headed for home.

On the way, they took in 175 tons of oil fuel at Aden and another 400 tons at Port Said. Some of the cargo was discharged in London and the remainder in Dunkirk.

Home on leave Dec 17th - 26th [Christmas!], rejoining the ship on 26th.

28 Dec 1929 - 5 April 1930 [over three months]: Travelled to the west coast of Africa, round the Cape of Good Hope, to ports on the east, returning – after taking in the island of

Mauritius in the Indian Ocean – through the Suez Canal and the Mediterranean:

Newport (River Severn, Wales), Glasgow, Birkenhead, Africa - Dakar, Durban, Lourenco Marques and Beira - then Mauritius (Port Louis), and through the Suez Canal, Suez and Port Said, home to Newport Mon.

The ship left Newport, bound for Glasgow, with a cargo of railway material. There was a following gale which delayed progress due to heavy rolling and a danger of the cargo shifting. "Abeam Smalls at midnight but forced to continue South-West at slow speed till 11am, when course was altered".

On arrival in Glasgow, Jack had another short leave, re-joining the ship on 3rd January.

The ship left Glasgow in a moderate southerly gale. Arrived Birkenhead on 5th January and loaded part general cargo. Continued to have gales and nasty weather for another week or so until off Teneriffe. In Dakar on 22nd January took on 700 tons of fuel oil - the process being delayed by a burst oil pipe. Then went to Durban and discharged part of the cargo, then to Lourenco Marques to discharge another 2000 tons and take on 1900 tons of bunkers. They discharged more cargo at Beira and the remaining cargo in Mauritius.

[It was nice to see that Jack had called in to Mauritius. On our way from England to Australia in 1975, to take up a job, we stopped for a few days in Mauritius. More recently, since they started their own airline, we have been to Mauritius a few times - it has become a favourite spot for the occasional holiday or for a few days' stopover on the way to or from the UK or Europe. I doubt if Jack got anywhere near a resort hotel or even if there were such things in Mauritius back then].

After that the ship was empty and returned to Newport via the Suez Canal.

Home on leave April 5th - 12th, re-joining at Avonmouth on 12th

Jan. 25th	½ fl. Capstan	4/2	
	2 bots. beer	6/-	
" 26	1 bot. whisky	6/6	owing from M.S.
" —	½ fl. Capstan	4/2	
" 30	3 bots beer	1/6	
Feb. 2	2 " "	1/0	
	1 bot. whisky	6/6	owing from M.S.
" 7	3 bots beer	2/6	
" 9	3 bots beer	2/0	
" 11	1 bot. whisky	6/6	owing from M.S.
	2 bots beer	1/0	
" 14th	3 " "	2/6	
1st 18 "		9/-	
" "	100 cigs	3/6	
Mar. 3rd	1 bot. whisky	praise 6/6/gin }	owing from M.S.
" 9th	do	6/6 } do	cancelled
" 10th	1 bot. gin	4/0	
	2 bots beer	1/0	
Mar 19th	1 bot whisky	6/6	owing from M.S.

Feb. 6th   Durban.   £5 . 0 . 0 .
Mar. 8th   Mauritius R⁵15 @ 14(?) : £1 . 1 . 3

Postage.   Durban   8/6   (2 Airmail)
           Beira   8ᵈ   (2)
           Mauritius 5ᵈ   (2)

~~cancelled~~
~~M.S.   L.t.   A.W.   L.d~~
from I.Etg   H.

Jack was well organised.

An advantage of being on ships is that your accommodation, cramped though it probably is, doesn't cost you anything.
Nor do your meals.
So there's nothing much to spend money on, except for tobacco and alcohol.
Even they were duty free.

I have no idea what he was paid.
But he kept track of what he was spending.

To the left is a typical page of his expenses notes, at around the time of this voyage – he spent money in Durban and bought some local currency for Mauritius.

I really like 6/6 for a bottle of whisky.
That's about 33p in decimal UK currency – something like 50 Australian cents at 60p per $A, a typical rate of exchange these days.

Beer was 6d a bottle – 2 bottles for 5p in decimal UK currency.

100 cigarettes cost 3/6 – about 18p.

There's been a lot of inflation in the last 90 years, of course, but at these prices I don't think he needed to stint himself. By the frequency of those 6/6s, I don't think he did.

12 April - 3 August 1930 [nearly four months]: A roughly similar trip round Africa from west to east, returning via the Suez Canal:

Avonmouth (River Severn), Glasgow and Birkenhead (River Mersey) to Africa - Dakar, Lobito, Cape Town, Mossel Bay, Port Elizabeth, East London, Lourenco Marques, Dar-es-Salaam, Tanga, Mombasa - then home via Suez and Port Said to Liverpool and Glasgow.

There was a rather hesitant start to this trip. It went to Glasgow to pick up cargo and bunkers and Jack had another short leave (14th-18th April) while it was there. The ship then called in to Birkenhead for a few days to load more cargo and Jack had another mini-leave (22nd-25th April). Then it got going properly.

Took in oil fuel at Dakar and then offloaded cargo in stages at the next few ports of call – Lobito, Cape Town, Mossel Bay, Port Elizabeth and finally East London.

Travelled empty to Lourenco Marques and took in 1000 tons of bunkers but carried on empty to Dar-es-Salaam to pick up some cargo. Loaded more cargo at Tanga and Mombasa ("hides, cotton-seed, oil cake etc").

On leaving Mombasa, trip planning jumped around a bit - originally they were bound for Djibouti but, when only 50 miles from there, at 4.00pm on 7th January, were diverted to Port Sudan. Five hours later, they were diverted to Suez direct. (And it notes "Very hot weather in Red Sea.")

They had a clear run through the Suez Canal, dropped a small amount of cargo at Port Said and took on fresh water there.

They were told by their owners, the Clan Line, to proceed at 10 knots to Liverpool, where they discharged most of the cargo before finishing the trip at Glasgow.

Home on leave 5th – 18th August.

18 August 1930 – 9 February 1931 [nearly six months]:
Glasgow, Barrow-in-Furness, Glasgow, Birkenhead, Lobito, Cape Town, Mossel Bay, Port Elizabeth, East London, Durban,

then to ports on Madagascar - Tulear, Morombe, Anbalahonko, Morombe, Morondava, Namangoa, Soarana, Morondava, Lovobe, Morondava, Magunga – then to the African coast ports of Dar-es-Salaam (with a loop back to Tulear, Madagascar), Beira, Tanga and Mombasa before returning via Djibouti, Port Sudan, Suez, Port Said and Algiers to London, Liverpool and Glasgow.

This trip started with a local side trip to Barrow (almost at home!) to pick up railway lines. Then they loaded more cargo in Glasgow and swung the ship to calibrate the compass. Next stop Birkenhead, to load more cargo including locomotives. Jack managed another mini holiday at home (25th -29th August) while the ship was in Birkenhead.

Two and a half weeks later they had arrived in Lobito, West Africa, to offload some cargo, including two locomotives, and they spent the next three and a half weeks calling in at southern African ports to discharge cargo, the last batch being offloaded at East London.

This voyage also took in ports in Madagascar. They travelled empty from East London and then picked up cargo at successive ports (beans, hides, mangrove bark, rafia...), with more cargo added at Dar-es-Salaam, Tulea(Madagascar), Beira, Tanga, Mombasa, Djibouti and (late diversion) Port Sudan. Christmas Day happened when heading for Djibouti and New Year's Day on the way to Suez. They then headed for home through the Suez Canal and called in at Algiers for bunkers, fresh water and another 50 tons of cargo.

In London (Tilbury Dock) they discharged some of the cargo but also loaded "transhipment cargo and stores" for Liverpool. Jack managed to take a few days leave (20th - 27th January) while the ship was in London. They had **gales on the way to Liverpool**, where they discharged more cargo and Jack took more leave (2nd - 6th February).

Finally, they went to Glasgow, **again in a gale.**

Left S/S Clan MacNair. Home on leave for only two days (10th - 11th February) and was then appointed to **S/S Clan MacIlwraith**, also owned by Clan Line and also in Glasgow.

S/S Clan MacIlwraith 14 February - 29 June 1931
[four and a half months]: From Britain and Europe the ship headed through the Mediterranean and Suez Canal to ports in south east India. Then it went to north-west India and made its way back, stopping along the way.

Map of India:page 89
Glasgow, Birkenhead, Middlesbrough, London, Antwerp (Germany), Oran and Port Said (Mediterranean), then India - Tuticorin, Allepey, Trivandrum, Cochin, Calicut, Beypore, Chittagong, Cocanada, Vizagapatam, Madras, Colombo, Tuticorin - returning via Aden, Suez, Port Said, Marseilles, Oran, London and Dunkirk (France) to Glasgow.

S/S Clan MacIlwraith
Built 1924
Gross Registered Tonnage 4838
Length 387 feet
Beam 52 feet
Horse Power 653: Steam driven piston engine with low pressure turbine. Fitted for oil firing as well as coal.

They had some cargo on leaving Glasgow and loaded more in Birkenhead, Middlesbrough, London and Antwerp (Belgium) before heading for Algeria (took on bunkers and fresh water in Oran) and through the Suez Canal to India. They discharged cargo at all ports up to Chittagong.

At Chittagong they started loading again - tea, followed by ground nuts at Cocanada, manganese ore at Vizagapatam and other cargo at ports up to Aden. In Aden they took in oil fuel.

Took in more fuel and some cargo at Port Said then travelled along and across the Mediterranean Sea to Marseilles (south of France) to offload some cargo. At Oran (Algeria) they took in bunkers [coal, which I find surprising] and 70 tons of cargo (fibre). The cargo was discharged in London and Dunkirk (northern France) with the remainder presumably going to the final port, Glasgow, where Jack left the ship.

96

Jack took a long session of leave, two months of it unpaid, from 1st July to 4th September, then signed on again on 5th September - this time to **S/S Lochbroom** - owned by MacBrayne and coasting the Scottish West Highlands out of Glasgow. Still very Scottish but quite a change from Africa and India. And quite a change of ship - to a little, sixty-year old island steamer.

RMS Lochbroom
Built 1871
Gross Registered Tonnage 1086
Length 242 feet
Beam 31 feet
Horse Power 262: Steam driven piston engine. Coal fired.

Like MacBrayne's S/S Clydesdale, this was a Royal Mail Ship (RMS) making similar trips round the evocative place names of the Scottish West Coast (see 13. Scottish Interlude on page 75).

The routes and calling places (most not big enough to be called a Port) were different, though. While RMS Clydesdale covered outer islands, RMS Lochbroom stuck mainly to the west coast of the mainland, though it took in the islands of Skye, Mull and Eigg. Because the calling places were so different, I've shown them separately on the two maps (page 76 for RMS Clydesdale and page 99 for RMS Lochbroom)

RMS Lochbroom: 5 August - 10 November 1931
[a little over three months]:
Map of Scotland RMS Lochbroom service:page 99

The trips were Glasgow to Glasgow, six in all. Most of them went like this: Glasgow, Greenock, Oban, Craignure, Lochaline, Salen, Tobermoray (Island of Mull), Eigg (Island), Armadale and Isle Ornsay (both on the Island of Skye, just across the Sound of Sleat from the mainland), Kyle of Lochalsh (where the road bridge to Skye has since been built), Broadford, Portree and Staffin (all on Skye), Gairloch,

Inverasdale, Aultbea and Scoraig (all around Loch Ewe), Ullapool, Baden Tarbert (now just called Tarbert: it's on the mainland - not the Tarbert on South Harris Island) then back again, calling at some of the same places.

On some trips they went a little further north to take in Loch Inchard, Loch Clash, Loch Laxford and (Loch) Nedd.

On the third trip the log says they had bad weather throughout and were delayed at Loch Inchard.

On the last trip, they called in at Loch Inver when returning south, before reaching Ullapool. Then they had to spend an extra day in Kyle of Lochalsh, sheltering from a gale. Well it was November by then, so not a time for idyllic weather.

For someone besotted with the Highlands and West Coast of Scotland (me), all this chugging around sounds delightful. Maybe being stuck with the repetition of it for three months was something else again. It works out at about a fortnight for each round trip, Glasgow to Glasgow. It obviously wasn't a speed boat.

It took passengers, though, and a couple of weeks being ferried around that beautiful scenery was probably very enjoyable. I'm pretty sure it was during this time that Jack met his wife to be (and my mother to be) having a holiday on board as a passenger.

RMS Lochbroom at Portree, Isle of Skye, 1931

LANDING PLACES AND PORTS
Islands

LOCH CLASH
LOCH INCHARD
LOCH LAXFORD
BADEN TARBERT
LOCH INVER
NEDD — BADCALL
ULLAPOOL
SCORAIG
INVERASDALE
ALTBEA
GAIRLOCH
STAFFIN
APPLECROSS
BROADFORD (*Skye*)
PORTREE
KYLE OF LOCHALSH
GLENELG
Skye
ARMADALE (*Skye*)
MALLAIG
ISLE ORNSAY
SALEN
Eigg
LOCHALINE
OBAN
TOBERMORAY
Mull
CRAIGNURE
GLASGOW

Scotland

River Clyde
GREENOCK

England

Scotland: West Coast and Islands RMS Lochbroom service

The story as he told it was that, while he was out on deck, this nearby female passenger "accidentally" dropped her ring and it rolled out of sight. She then effected distress at its loss. So he had to obligingly scrabble around and find it for her.

Well maybe it wasn't quite like that but, whether it was or not, it worked!

I knew they met on a MacBrayne's steamer on the west coast of Scotland but have had to deduce that it was this one. Mercia, for that's who it was, would have been widowed for nearly two years by then. And maybe the notion I had that the cruise was a present from her father when she qualified as a nurse isn't right, because the timing doesn't work. I still think it was a present from him, but maybe just a nice thing to do for his daughter after the difficult time she had been through. She would have been starting, not finishing, her training as a nurse.

Jack left S/S Lochbroom after finishing his sixth voyage with her, to rejoin his old ship **S/S Clan MacNair** two days later. He was back to the longer, warmer voyages typical of the Clan Line.

S/S Clan MacNair 14 November 1931 to 3 March 1932 [three and a half months]:

Maps: Home(Britain):pages 6/7 Mediterranean:pages 20/21 Middle East:page 25 Africa;page 88 India:page 89

Through the Suez Canal to India (and Ceylon):
Glasgow, Birkenhead, Port Said, Suez, Colombo, Madras, Calcutta, Chittagong, Bunlipatam/Madras, Colombo, Tutucorin, Aden, Suez, Port Said, London, Dundee, Glasgow.

This seems to have been a fairly routine trip - cargo taken from UK to Colombo (Ceylon, now Sri Lanka) and the Indian ports en route to Chittagong. At Chittagong and subsequent Indian ports up to Tuticorin they progressively added cargo to deliver to London, Dundee and Glasgow. They took in oil fuel at Aden and Port Said on the way home but there is no other mention of bunkers, stores or water for this relatively modern ship.

Near the end of the voyage, Jack managed to take a few days leave (18th - 24th February) while the ship was docked in London. It then went to Glasgow via Dundee so rounded the north of Scotland. In Glasgow the ship was drydocked for a couple of days and it discharged its remaining cargo, part loaded new cargo and took in bunkers. Home on leave again 8th - 12th March, returning to the same ship.

[Interestingly, he mentions being in Newcastle for two days during this leave. It follows logically from having met Mercia, his future wife and my future mother, when she was cruising on RMS Lochbroom. She would probably have been training as a nurse, in Newcastle, in March 1932.]

S/S Clan MacNair 12 March - 24 June 1932
[three and a half months]:
Map of Africa:page 88

Down the west coast of Africa, round the cape and returning through the Suez Canal:
Glasgow, Birkenhead, Durban, Lourenco Marques, Beira, Dar-es-Salaam, Mombasa, Port Sudan, Suez, Port Said, Avonmouth, Liverpool, Glasgow.

This trip was also apparently routine, though there was some minor engine trouble. They took outward cargo from Glasgow and Birkenhead to be offloaded in Durban, Lourenco Marques and, finally, Beira. Then they picked up cargo in Dar-es-Salaam, Mombasa and Port Sudan (cotton in bags) to offload in Liverpool and Glasgow (no mention of cargo at Avonmouth). They also took some coastal cargo from Liverpool to Glasgow.

Jack managed a few days leave near the start of the voyage (14th - 18th March) and also near the end (18th - 22nd June) while the ship was docked in Birkenhead. As an experienced sea dog, it seems he had got the knack of getting clear of the ship when it was docked near home.

On the way from Birkenhead to Durban, they stopped off at Sierra Leone with a broken "eccentric strap on the Low Pressure Cylinder". They had a spare or were able to repair it or do without it, but they lost a few hours.

After leaving Durban they had "trouble in engine room with hot rod, and several short stops in the morning."

At Beira they used shore cranes to transfer coal from a hold to bunkers. It's interesting that the ship could use both coal and oil as fuel - and that they were using unused cargo space to carry extra coal fuel and presumably give them more range. The only other mention of fuel is that they took in oil at Port Said on the way home.

Home on leave, 27th June to 7th July, then rejoined the ship at Glasgow.

9 July - 21 October 1932 [three and a half months]: to India and back through the Suez Canal:
Glasgow, Swansea, Birkenhead (on leave 13 th- 15th July), Port Said, Colombo, Madras, Calcutta, Chittagong, Madras, Colombo, Tuticorin, Aden, Suez, Port Said, London (on leave 8th - 13th Oct), Dundee (on leave 16th - 18th Oct), Glasgow.

Maps: Home (Britain):pages 6/7   Mediterranean:pages 20/21
Middle East:page 25   India:page 89

Nothing dramatic but some difficult weather on this trip. They loaded cement in Swansea, presumably loaded more cargo in Birkenhead (while Jack was on leave) then headed for Ceylon and India via the Suez Canal, taking in a little cargo at Port Said and then offloading cargo at successive ports to Chittagong - though they also loaded some cargo at Madras. They also took on successive amounts of cargo from Chittagong (tea and jute) and following ports to Tuticorin.

102

Unusually, they discharged some cargo at Port Said but most was discharged at London and Dundee (final leg to Glasgow being empty). In London, part of the ad hoc nature of the trade, they loaded jute which had been brought in on the sister ship S/S Clan Sinclair, to deliver to Dundee.

In Calcutta, alongside the coal berth, they took in 600 tons of bunkers. At Aden and at Port Said, on the way home, they took in oil fuel. Definitely a dual-fuel ship. Presumably, they used whatever fuel cost less and was conveniently available. It must have helped the economics.

Weather was less than ideal from the start. On the first day out, in mid-summer, they had fog on the way from Glasgow to Swansea. A few days after leaving Suez they encountered **a strong South-West monsoon wind. There was also a heavy South-Westerly swell. The vessel was shipping water and rolling heavily. Again, after leaving Madras, progress was delayed by a strong South-Westerly wind and heavy South-Westerly swell. There was fog in the Suez Canal** on the way home, which delayed them.

Jack left the S/S Clan MacNair in Glasgow and was home on unpaid leave from 25th October to 11th November. Then he joined **S/S Cordillera** - owned by Donaldson SA Line - in Glasgow.

Buenos Aries - Central Railway Station

Buenos Aries -Avenida de Mayo

16. More Globe Trotting

Maps: Home(Britain):pages 6/7   Northern Europe:page 35
Africa:page 88   South America:page 81   Asia-Australia:page 28

S/S Cordillera 11 November 1932 - 31 January 1933

[11 weeks]:   Initially down the west coast of Africa, then roughly south and a little west to South America:
Glasgow, Liverpool, St Vincent CV (Cape Verde), Montevideo, Buenos Aries/La Blanca, La Plata, Montevideo, Liverpool

S/S Cordillera
Built 1920
Gross Registered Tonnage 6865
Length 419 feet
Beam 45 feet
Horse Power 756: Steam turbines - both oil and coal burning.

Another advance in technology - purely turbine driven and no pistons. Again, they had the flexibility of using either oil or coal to raise steam.

The trip was relatively short, taking cargo from Liverpool to Montevideo and Buenos Aries. The inclusion of St Vincent, Cape Verde Islands, on the outward voyage was as a refuelling stop - 1170 tons of oil. It then took nearly two weeks to get to Montevideo to discharge some cargo. At Buenos Aries they discharged the remaining outward cargo. There and at La Plata they loaded frozen and chilled meat and they finalised loading cargo at Montevideo, taking it to Liverpool.

Liverpool and the Mersey were a little unkind: there was dense fog there at the beginning of the voyage and fog again on arriving back. They were also delayed on the last few days of the voyage by a heavy north-easterly gale [blowing against them].

Four days of leave (31st January - 3rd February) at home, then rejoined the ship at Liverpool.

4 February - 13 June 1933 [over four months]:

To Australia and back via the west coast of Africa.

Liverpool, Las Palmas, Canary Islands (to load 1200 tons of oil bunkers), then headed south and east to round the Cape of Good Hope and cross the Indian Ocean to Australia. First stop was Melbourne, returning via the Western Australian ports of Albany and Fremantle. Then across the Indian Ocean again to Cape Town (to load 100 tons of oil bunkers), rounding the Cape and heading to Dakar on the West African coast (another 600 tons of oil fuel) and then to London (Royal Alfred Dock), Hamburg (Germany), Hull (east coast of England) and Glasgow.

This summary covers a surprisingly long trip with a nasty end to it.

Initially, they took on 2600 tons of coal bunkers and loaded dunnage wood [used to secure cargo in place]. Then they set sail, with no cargo, on 8th February but were delayed leaving, waiting for a doctor for an injured man. Unusually, they travelled empty half way round the world to Melbourne, stopping only to take on fuel.

In Australia, they loaded fruit. In Melbourne, 104000 cases of apples and 21000 cases of pears. In Albany, 20000 cases of apples and, in Fremantle, 30000 cases of apples and pears. Then they sailed back, stopping only for fuel, and discharged cargo at Hamburg and Hull.

It doesn't say anything about discharging cargo in London, where they called before heading for Hamburg, but maybe mention of that was overlooked by **a rather nasty incident in London: on their way up river they collided with S/S Royal Archer. This did considerable damage to the poop [back deck] and forecastle [front deck] and it carried away 30 feet of the starboard side of S/S Royal Archer. Worse, a passenger was killed and another badly injured.**

I was very pleased to see that Jack had called in at Albany, a favourite holiday place of ours, and Fremantle, the local port for Perth, where we have lived for over forty years. I'm afraid Western Australia wasn't very welcoming. On the way from Albany to Fremantle, in early April (so Autumn weather, not winter) progress was delayed by a heavy westerly gale and rough seas. This gale continued as they passed Cape Leeuwin and, when off Fremantle, the weather was too severe for them to enter the roads and anchor.

They had to stand off and on all night before they could enter the harbour and berth. A week after leaving Fremantle, crossing the Indian Ocean, they had more strong winds (South South West) and heavy seas, which much reduced their speed.

Sorry, Jack!

The end of the trip had them offloading cargo at Hull on the east coast of England, then ending the voyage at Glasgow on the west coast of Scotalnd - so it would have been another passage round the north of Scotland/Great Britain.

At the end of this long voyage, Jack went home on unpaid leave for about six weeks, from 14th June - 3rd August 1933.

Then he was appointed to **S/S Clan MacIndoe** (Clan Line again) berthed in Glasgow and loading general cargo for Calcutta.

17. India Again

Maps: Home(Britain):pages 6/7   Middle East:page 25
India (and Ceylon):page 89

S/S Clan Macindoe 5 August - 14 November 1933
[three and a half months]:
Glasgow, Birkenhead (home on leave four days), through the
Mediterranean to Port Said and the Suez Canal, then
Colombo, Madras, Calcutta, Chittagong and Colombo again,
returning via Aden, Suez and Port Said to London, Dundee,
Greenock and Glasgow.

S/S Clan MacIndoe
Built 1920
Gross Registered Tonnage 4635
Length 385 feet
Beam 52 feet
Horse Power 613: Steam driven piston engine with low
pressure turbine. Fitted for oil firing as well as coal.

This was fairly typical of the other Clan Line trips to
India and Ceylon (now Sri Lanka), and uneventful. They took
general cargo from Glasgow (and presumably from
Birkenhead) and discharged it successively at Colombo,
Madras, Calcutta and Chittagong. They also carried a small
consignment from Colombo to Chittagong and took 300 tons
of coal (bunkers for sister ship S/S Clan Murdoch) from
Calcutta to Chittagong. At Chittagong they took in a full return
cargo of tea and jute.

They discharged the tea in London, loaded a
transhipment of more jute and delivered all the jute to
Dundee. The ship then rounded the north of Scotland to go
briefly into dry dock in Greenock before docking in Glasgow.

On the way out, they refuelled with 350 tons of coal in
Calcutta. Returning, they took in 230 tons of bunkers at

Colombo and oil fuel at Aden and Port Said (where they also tookin fresh water).

Jack left this ship at Glasgow after only one voyage.
Home on unpaid leave, 15th - 26th November. [Unpaid leave is being increasingly common in these later years. Perhaps he was just enjoying more leave and was sufficiently cashed up to be able to take it on his own time.]

Joined **S/S City of Sydney** (Hall Line) in Glasgow. This was bound for Calcutta via Birkenhead, taking general cargo, but Jack was only on the ship for the two days from Glasgow to Birkenhead, then he signed on to **S/S Baron Tweedmouth** at nearby Liverpool. This, too, was short-lived.

S/S Baron Tweedmouth left Liverpool (north west England) on 30th November 1933 bound for the Tyne (north east England) via the south coast and English Channel. **They found themselves heading into gales - southerly as they headed south, then easterly when they rounded Lands End. At this point, progress was very slow. Trouble developed in the engine room and they had to put back into West Bay, Portland, for shelter and temporary repairs. They anchored there for two days and then, in better weather, proceeded at reduced speed (due to the temporary nature of the repairs).**
On arrival at the Tyne (8th December) the ship went into dry dock and Jack took annual leave. He had intended to be on leave until 31st December but was recalled on 22nd and appointed to **S/S Homeside** at Dunstan Staithes [on the river Tyne], loading coal for Gibraltar. This ship had a different owner - a Newcastle company, Charlton McAllum and Co.

18. A Bit Rough

Maps: Home(Britain):pages 6/7 Northern Europe:page 35
South America:page 81 Africa:page 88

S/S Homeside 23 December 1933 - 24 March 1934
[three months]:
Dunstan (River Tyne), Gibraltar, then south to the east coast
of South America (Buenos Aries roads and Rosario), calling at
St Vincent (Cape Verde Islands) on the return trip to
Falmouth and Birkenhead.

S/S Homeside Built 1924 Gross Registered Tonnage 4617 Length 384 feet Beam 52 feet Horse Power 406: Steam driven piston engine.

This seems to have been a rough trip in terms of weather
and it was also a little hand-to-mouth for cargoes and
destinations. The initial trip to Gibraltar, carrying coal, had
been set up and was straightforward, though they ran into a
south-westerly gale in the Bay of Biscay and had to heave to.
After Gibraltar they headed, without cargo, towards South
America awaiting orders. They anchored in Buenos Aries
roads and were finally ordered to nearby Rosario to pick up a
full cargo of wheat. They then headed roughly north over the
South Atlantic, then North Atlantic, to Vincent on the Cape
Verde Islands, for bunkers and orders - but they had strong
head winds and slow progress. They were then ordered to go
to Birkenhead.

Off Madeira (north of Cape Verde Islands), there was a
northerly gale and "progress much delayed". After four days
of this, [they must have been using more fuel than planned]
"Finally necessary to put into Falmouth for bunkers." Another

four days after that, they put into Falmouth and took in 50 tons of bunkers. "Bunkering delayed by bad weather."

On reaching Birkenhead and discharging the cargo, the ship shifted to Cammel Lairds Dry Dock for painting and repairs "(damage by weather homeward bound.)"

Home on leave for four days (24th - 28th March), rejoining at the Dry Dock, then:

29 - 31 March 1934: Birkenhead to Cardiff (light ship). Signed off and was home on leave for over a fortnight, to 16th April.

Appointed to **S/S Holtby** on 16th April, at Cardiff, loaded with coal, awaiting the opening of the St Lawrence Seaway [after its normal iced-up closure during the winter].

S/S Holtby 17 April - 12 June 1934 [eight weeks]:
Cardiff, Montreal, London, Swansea
>   *Maps: Home(Britain):pages 6/7   Canada:page 12*

S/S Holtby
Built 1909
Gross Registered Tonnage 3681
Length 347 feet
Beam 54 feet
Horse Power 301: Steam driven piston engine.

A straightforward trip but not the best weather conditions. The voyage started with "strong head gales and progress very slow." The gales continued for over a week. They then sighted icebergs but the weather was "generally fine and clear in the ice-track", though there were occasional snow showers and fog patches. The direct route in the St Lawrence Seaway was closed by pack ice so they had to

112

divert round it. In Montreal they discharged the coal cargo and loaded a full cargo of grain, the whole process taking about a week. On the way back, the direct route was clear of ice so they took it. Off Cape Race "Considerable ice sighted between 50 and 44 degrees west. Fog patches. Otherwise fine weather."

While the ship was in London, Jack took three days' leave at home, then rejoined the ship on its way to Swansea (no cargo). Then he left the ship and was home on leave again from 13th - 25th June.

Appointed to S/S Fishpool on 25th June, loading coal at Swansea.

S/S Fishpool 25 June - 13 August 1934 [six weeks]:
Swansea, Montreal, Wabana (Newfoundland), Emden (Netherlands), Swansea.
    Maps: Canada:page12   Northern Europe:page 35

S/S Fishpool
Built 1912
Gross Registered Tonnage 4575
Length 379 feet
Beam 56 feet
Horse Power 380: Steam driven piston engine.

This was another straightforward trip, though hardly a balmy cruise. Ten days into the voyage they had strong head winds and fog patches. Three days later it had become a **strong north-westerly gale with rain and mist**. It then cleared but there was **"some ice"**. At Montreal, they discharged the coal cargo but then travelled light for a week on the way to Wabana, Newfoundland. Again the weather was challenging: three days out of Montreal there was **"dense fog and a strong SW gale."**

The dense fog persisted for another two days and, shortly before arriving at Wabana they **"stopped on account of ice."** At Wabana they loaded a full cargo of Iron Ore. When they left Wabana, they had to stop for 7 hours during the night "on account of ice in the vicinity". Apart from a southerly gale on 1st August it was then reasonable weather.

Emden involves going up the river Ems and passing through locks. They had a delay because a wire parted when going through the locks, injuring a sailor.

Having offloaded the iron ore at Emden, the ship travelled light to Swansea but had slow progress initially because of a South West gale in the North Sea. After passing the Lizard they had to stop for an hour in the night for engine room repairs.

The voyage finished on 13th August and Jack went home on leave from 15th - 21st, rejoining the ship at the end of that, still in Swansea and loading a full cargo of coal ready for a repeat performance.

24 August - 20 October 1934 [eight weeks]: Swansea, Montreal, Newfoundland Ports (Traytown, Halls Bay and Middle Arm Green Bay, all on the north coast), Swansea, Cardiff.

The outward voyage, much like the last one, took coal from Swansea to Montreal. They then travelled light to Newfoundland, three different ports this time, to progressively pick up cargo - pit props - an appropriate cargo to take back to the mining area of South Wales, served by Swansea.

Weather was again unwelcoming. For the first week, there were strong gales turning from south to south-east to north-west. At one stage they had to heave to for several hours. Then they had two separate days with dense fog. There were more days of fog between Montreal and Newfoundland.

Fog delayed them leaving Traytown, Newfoundland. Finally, there was bad weather for three days after leaving Newfoundland. All well apart from that, except there weren't enough pit-props to give them a full cargo and they left for home with 3250 tons of cargo capacity unused, which probably didn't help the trip's profitability.

At the end of the voyage the ship left Swansea on a Friday, arriving in Cardiff on the Saturday. Jack signed off but remained on the ship for the weekend.

On the Monday he was appointed to **S/S Glitra** which was discharging its cargo at Sharpness [on the River Severn]. He travelled on this ship to Swansea, arriving on the evening of 24th October, then left the ship.

Appointed on 25th October to **S/S Euphorbia**, also at Swansea, which was loading a full cargo of coal.

19. America Again, with Side Trips

Maps: Home(Britain):pages 6/7
USA:page 50   Cuba:page 72

S/S Euphorbia 27 October 1934 - 31 January 1935
[three months]: From Swansea, across the Atlantic to
Boston, Lynn (Mass.) and Boston again. Then to Cuba – the
Guantanamo Bay ports of Boqueron and Caimanera. Back to
USA - New York (Edgewater and Brooklyn), Portsmouth
(New Hampshire) and New York again. Then back across the
Atlantic to Ardrossan on the west coast of Scotland.

S/S Euphorbia Built 1924 Gross Registered Tonnage 3380 Length 331 feet Beam 48 feet Horse Power 249: Steam driven piston engine.

Carried coal from Swansea to Boston and nearby Lynn.
Then had a change of charterer. Headed for Cuba with no
cargo and loaded sugar at the two ports in Guantanamo Bay
(about 5300 tons altogether). The sugar was mostly bound
for Edgewater with the balance to Brooklyn (about 10 miles
apart in New York).

Travelled light to Portsmouth, New Hampshire, and
loaded 1650 tons of scrap iron using a magnet (worked day
and night, except Christmas Day). At New York they loaded
more scrap iron taking them up to a full cargo of about 5100
tons. Loading in New York was delayed since the cargo was
held up by dense fog. Then they carried the cargo to
Ardrossan [North Ayrshire on the west coast of Scotland].

There was more bad weather this trip. There was a
**heavy gale blowing when they left Swansea and they
anchored in shelter**. On the way in to New York after
leaving Cuba there were more gales. They lost a day
unloading sugar in Brooklyn because of rain. When they left

117

Portsmouth, New Hampshire (8.00am on New Year's Day) they were **"compelled to anchor outside harbour owing to blizzard."** They set off again at 3.45pm **in "heavy North West gale. Rolling terrifically".**

Finally, they anchored off Ardrossan waiting for the tide but were "unable to dock on this tide owing to **dense fog**."

Jack left this ship on 31st January and took three weeks unpaid leave.

On 21st February, he was appointed to **S/S Clan MacNab** at Glasgow, which was loading general cargo.

20. Jobbing around Africa and India with a bit of USA

Maps: Home(Britain):pages 6/7 Africa:page 88 USA:page 50
India:page 89 Middle East:page 28 Northern Europe:page 35

S/S Clan MacNab 22 February - 16 October 1935

[nearly eight months]: Down the west coast of Africa and round the Cape of Good Hope, then north to Beira on the east coast of Africa. Returning south from there, back round the Cape, and across the South Atlantic to southern and eastern USA. Another reversal to go round the Cape once more, to ports on the east coast of southern Africa, and then roughly north-east to India, returning home through the Suez Canal:

Glasgow, Liverpool (took 5 days leave while the ship was here), Durban, Lourenco Marques, Beira, Cape Town, Dakar, Galveston, Philadelphia, New York, Cape Town, Port Elizabeth, East London, Durban, Lourenco Marques, Beira, Indian ports - Marmagoa, Cochin, Alleppey, Galle and Marmagoa again - returning through Aden, Suez, Port Said, London Tilbury, Hamburg (Germany), Antwerp (Belgium) and Greenock (went into dry dock) to Glasgow.

S/S Clan MacNab
Built 1920
Gross Registered Tonnage 6117
Length 411 feet
Beam 53 feet
Horse Power 692: Steam driven piston engine with low pressure turbine. Fitted for oil firing as well as coal.

This fairly long voyage had a family resemblance to earlier trips with the Clan Line - based on Glasgow, picking up Africa and India and, on the return only this time, going through the Suez Canal.

They started by taking general cargo from Glasgow and Liverpool. Part of this, including some locomotives, was discharged at Durban in South Africa where they also loaded 5000 cases of case-oil (petrol). They discharged the remaining cargo at Lourenco Marques and Beira.

At Beira they loaded a full cargo of maize from railway trucks. Took in oil bunkers at Cape Town (65 tons) and Dakar (760 tons) [presumably it was cheaper at Dakar but they needed fuel by Cape Town so had to buy some].

They didn't initially have orders about where to take the maize but had a radio message to go to Galveston, USA. They worked day and night in Galveston to discharge this cargo, then fumigated the ship. That all took about a week.

They left Galveston with no cargo. On the way to Philadelphia they had to stop twice with engine trouble. At Philadelphia they loaded a part cargo of case-oil then, in New York, loaded some general cargo and also took in both coal and oil bunkers.

They dropped their cargo off in stages, all the way to Beira (where the last of it was offloaded). At Lourenco Marques, part way through this, they took in 800 tons of coal bunkers. After Beira, with no cargo, they headed for India.

At Marmagoa they loaded chrome ore - a bit different to the normal loads - then loaded more cargo successively at Cochin, Alleppey, Galle and Marmagoa (again). Heading home, at Aden and Port Said they took in oil fuel. They also discharged some cargo (unspecified) at Port Said but most of it was offloaded successively in London, Hamburg and Antwerp. The ship travelled empty from Antwerp to Greenock (three days in dry dock) and Glasgow.

Weather on the whole was unremarkable but, on leaving India bound for Aden, the monsoon was strong and slowed them down. Off Finisterre and Ushant, heading for London, there were several hours of fog. And on leaving London, headed for Hamburg, there was "considerable fog in the North Sea." Leaving Antwerp and heading along the Channel there was a "strong South West gale and head sea."

Jack went home on leave (via Newcastle, it says, so it seems that Mercia was definitely of interest by then) 18th - 31st October. He signed on again to this same ship, still at Glasgow and loading cargo, on 1st November.

1 November 1935 - 9 February 1936 [over three months]:
Glasgow, Liverpool (took leave while ship docked, 4th - 8th November), Dakar on the west coast of Africa (loaded 500 tons oil bunkers), then round the Cape of Good Hope to Durban, Lourenco Marques (took in coal bunkers), Beira, Dar-es-Salaam, Zanzibar, Tanga, Mombasa (fire!), Aden (took in 70 tons oil bunkers), Suez, Port Said (took in 700 tons of oil bunkers and fresh water), Liverpool (went home, Tuesday - Friday while ship docked), Glasgow.

The voyage started with general cargo loaded at Glasgow and Liverpool taken to Durban, Lourenco Marques and Beira. There were also a couple of smaller, probably opportunistic, cargo movements - at Durban they loaded a small amount of case-oil to take to Beira; and at Lourenco Marques they took some transhipment cargo ex S/S Hesione.

Fire!

The routine was definitely broken in Mombasa, with a difficult start to 1936.

"Fire breaks out Dec 31st (6 hours before due to sail) in cargo (sisal and cotton seed) contained in the bunker space on the starboard side, beneath accommodation.

A steam hose was put down the trunkway from the boat deck and hatches were covered. The vessel was taken out to anchor.

The trunkway was opened up next morning (New Years Day) and the water hose turned on but it was ineffective.

Tug came alongside and burst the portholes in the ship's side. Then hoses were put in from the tug and the fire was got under control and eventually extinguished.

There was slight damage to the accommodation.

The vessel came alongside [the quay] again at 9.00am Jan 2nd. Cargo discharged from bunker space (port and starboard) and some from No. 3 hold. Ship surveyed and damage repaired. Loading completed.

Left Mombasa 10.00am Jan 7th."

[So that delayed them a week.]

There was no cargo between Beira and Dar-es-Salaam then they loaded in steps at Dar-es-Salaam (about 700 tons of cotton, cotton seed, sisal and oilcake), Tanga and Mombasa (sisal, cotton seed etc) to take to Liverpool and Glasgow.

On the whole, the weather behaved itself but there were a couple of instances when it didn't.

On the way from Dakar to Durban there was a heavy head swell and fresh head winds. "Speed considerably reduced." And through the Mediterranean, on the way home, there were a couple of days with strong head winds, high swell and rough sea.

At the end of the voyage, in Glasgow, Jack went on leave from Monday 10th Feb to Saturday 15th, "(Newcastle Wed - Fri)". Still interested in that nurse, it seems.

Jack and Mercia

Then he rejoined the ship, still at Glasgow and loading for Colombo, Calcutta etc.

16 February - 1 June 1936 [three and a half months] :
Glasgow (adjusted compasses), Liverpool (home Tuesday pm to Friday am while the ship was in dock), Port Said, Aden (to transfer the Mate to Hospital), Colombo, Madras, Vizigapatam, Calcutta (loaded 800 tons coal bunkers), Chittagong, Bunlipatam , Vizigapatam, Masulipatam, Madras, Colombo, Tuticorim, Aden (took in oil bunkers), Suez, Port Said (took in oil fuel), London (on leave, 15th to 19th May,

while the ship was in dock), Dunkirk (northern France), Newport, Swansea, Glasgow.

This was mostly familiar territory from earlier voyages with Clan Line. Again, it was a jobbing cargo run. In Liverpool they loaded locomotives, bound for Chittagong (India). General cargo went to Colombo, Madras, Vizigapatam, Calcutta and Chittagong. Overlapping with this they loaded 1500 tons of pig iron at Calcutta and other cargo at Chittagong and following ports: Bunlipatam (500 tons of ground nuts), Vizigapatam (jute), Masulipatam (1000 tons of ground nuts), Madras (granite and hides) and Tuticorim (tea and jute), all bound for London and Dunkirk. At Newport and Swansea they loaded more general cargo to take to Glasgow.

Weather started badly, with thick fog all the way from Glasgow to Liverpool delaying progress and they had to go dead slow in the Mersey river. There was a heavy North East gale for two days in the Mediterranean and trouble with deck cargo (oil tanks), adding to delays.

At Port Said they were delayed for some hours for repairs in the engine room. There were no further weather problems around Ceylon and India but, on the way back, there was a moderate sand storm in the Suez Canal.

Passing through the Mediterranean on the way home they had to reduce speed for 12 hours because of a strong head gale and heavy seas. Finally, they hit bad weather going from London to Dunkirk. There was a strong gale. They had to anchor outside the port at Dunkirk for a few hours until the weather eased enough for them to get into the lock.

At the end of this voyage, Jack took leave from 2nd to 5th June, in Sunderland (well that's where she lived when not nursing!). He rejoined the ship then, still in Glasgow, loading cargo.

6 June - 27 September 1936 [nearly four months]:

Maps: Home(Britain):pages 6/7   Middle East:page 25
India(and Ceylon):page 89

Glasgow, Liverpool (home on leave, Mon - Fri, while ship in dock), Port Said, Suez, Colombo, Madras, Calcutta (took in coal bunkers), Chittagong, Madras, Colombo, Tuticorim, Aden (took in oil bunkers and fresh water), Suez, Port Said (took in oil bunkers), London Tilbury (home on leave pm 5th to am 11th, while ship is in dock), Swansea (on leave in Sunderland, 16th - 21st September while ship is in dock), Newport, Glasgow.

Initial cargo, from Glasgow and Liverpool, was supplemented by 600 tons of asphalt loaded at Suez.

They offloaded cargo successively at Colombo, Madras, Calcutta and Chittagong. But they also loaded cargo at Calcutta (2000 tons of pig iron) and Chittagong (tea and jute).

On the return trip they loaded more cargo at Madras, Colombo and, finally, Tuticorim though, in Aden, they also loaded a small consignment of mother-of-pearl.

Some repairs were needed in the engine room so they had to stop for about three hours on the way home near Cape St Vincent after leaving the Mediterranean.

The cargo was discharged in London and Swansea but they then did a little coastal work. In Swansea, they loaded 200 tons of cargo to be transhipped in Glasgow and they called in at Newport to load more cargo, all for Glasgow.

There was very little notable weather. About a week after leaving Suez they encountered a very strong south-west monsoon wind and swell, lasting three or four days. And there were some fog patches when travelling from London to Swansea, so they had to reduce speed and stop briefly.

At the end of the voyage, Jack took leave (in Sunderland again) from 29th September to 2nd October, then rejoined the ship, still at Glasgow and loading.

3 October 1936 - 13 January 1937
[about three and a half months]:

Map of Africa:page 88

Glasgow (swung ship to adjust compasses), Liverpool (took four days leave while the ship was docked here) then Africa - Cape Town, Mossel Bay, Port Elizabeth, East London, Durban, (Port Louis, Mauritius), Cape Town and Dakar - returning to London, Greenock (spent a day in dry dock) and Glasgow.

This voyage took (unspecified) cargo from Glasgow and Liverpool to be offloaded at Cape Town, Port Elizabeth and, finally, East London. They travelled light to Mauritius, calling in at Durban to take on 400 tons of bunkers.

Nice to see him calling in again at one of my favourite places, Mauritius, with mention of passing nearby Reunion Island, another memorable spot.

They loaded a full cargo of sugar in Mauritius along with small parcels of rum, copra and fibre, to take to London. En route, they stopped at Cape Town to take in bunkers and fresh water and at Dakar to take in oil, coal and water. The ship was empty for the final stage to Glasgow.

The weather seems to have been unremarkable on the whole but with some unpleasant patches. They encountered a gale and a quartering sea in the Bay of Biscay on the way out. There was heavy rain in East London which held up the discharging of cargo, and from East London to Durban they had a westerly gale with frequent heavy squalls and torrential rain. On the way to Cape Town, they met a strong westerly gale again, and high seas.

Jack left this ship at Glasgow and had a week's leave at home (via Sunderland: no doubt to see Mercia).

125

East London - Esplanade and Beach Hotel

21. Motoring Abroad

Maps: Home(Britain):pages 6/7   Middle East:page 25
Northern Europe:page 35   South America:page 81

On 22nd January 1937, Jack joined **MV British Union** at Wallsend-on-Tyne where it had been undergoing an overhaul.

MV British Union
Built 1927
Gross Registered Tonnage 6987
Length 440 feet
Beam 57 feet
Horse Power 749: A Motor Vessel: 6 cylinder diesel.

For the first time, we are without steam.   Not so much technical progress in itself, but a change of technology.

A piston engined diesel is more efficient than a piston engined steam engine, both in the power you get out of a given size of machine and in fuel efficiency.   (For large amounts of power, multi-stage steam turbines are still the go. That's what power stations still use and, until fairly recently, it was the technology of choice for fast liners and large military ships.)

Diesels are reliant on oil as a fuel, not coal, but the trend was away from coal anyway.

As a ship to navigate and to work the radio on, the type of engine probably made little difference.   Maybe it was slightly faster.   Almost certainly, it would have cost less to run.

MV British Union, 23 January - 30 March 1937
[nearly 10 weeks]:   Wallsend-on-Tyne, Port Said (took in stores), Suez (took in oil fuel), Abadan in the Persian Gulf (to load), Suez, Port Said then to Norway (Kristiansands and Oslo) and home to Grangemouth on the River Forth, east Scotland (stopped for four hours cleaning tanks).

They travelled light on the outward voyage ("Very heavy South East gale in Bay of Biscay") to load a full cargo in Abadan - of diesel oil, gas oil and furnace oil - bound for Kristiansands and Oslo in Norway. They also took in bunkers there. There were strong southerly winds and a rough sea on leaving Abadan and they had to anchor outside Shatt-al-Arab waiting for the weather to moderate so they could drop off the pilot. They were delayed in Suez owing to a sand storm in the canal. The final leg from Oslo to Grangemouth was in ballast (i.e. no cargo).

Jack continued on the ship without a break, initially for a local delivery:

1 April - 12 June 1937 [10 weeks]:
Grangemouth/Edinburgh (loaded full cargo, 10000 tons; departure delayed 12 hours due to damage to lock gates; foggy weather in North Sea)
to Purfleet in the River Thames (discharged 7000 tons, anchored in river - dense fog),
Hamble on south coast of England (fog in Channel, discharged remaining 3000 tons and proceeded in ballast) then to
Port Said (delayed by engine room repairs then delayed in transit on the canal due to Haitian ship aground),
Suez (took in bunkers from oil barge),
Abadan (took in full cargo of gas oil, diesel oil and fuel oil and took in bunkers) and
Aden ("discharged 3000 tons and loaded same amount."),
returning through Suez and Port Said to
Copenhagen (some fog on the way in, discharged 8000 tons),
Esbjerg (discharged remaining 2000 tons of cargo)and
River Tyne (berthed at Wallsend slipway for engine repairs).

Jack left this ship and had a couple of days leave at home before returning to Newcastle to join **S/S Bachaquero** (an oil tanker owned by Standard Oil) which was fitting out at High Shields. A new ship for a change: still a small one but with the sophistication of twin screws.

S/S Bachaquero
Built 1937
Gross Registered Tonnage 4890
Length 371 feet
Beam 64 feet
Horse Power 551: Steam driven piston engines, twin screws.

On 18th June, they had trials off Tynemouth all day, returning to Wallsend-on-Tyne. On 19th, minor adjustments were made in the engine room, the ship was handed over to its new crew and they loaded stores for the voyage.

Map of South America:page 81
S/S Bachaquero 20 June - 11 July 1937 [three weeks]:
Left Wallsend-on-Tyne (in ballast, no cargo) for South America – Aruba island off Venezuala, then Maracaibo and nearby La Salines (loaded full cargo of crude oil) and back to San Nicolas, Aruba (discharged cargo).

Jack was paid off and left this ship at Aruba, with a rather unusual month to follow. He wrote:

"Stayed in bachelors quarters, San Nicolas, until July 14th, awaiting repatriation at owners' expense. Left San Nicolas by car 9pm 14th and joined Dutch S/S Libertador at Oranjestad [capital of Aruba]. Left there 11.30pm for Curacao [Venezuela] and arrived there 9.00am 15th. Transferred to Dutch S/S Columbia (Royal Netherlands S.I.C.) and left Curacao midnight 15th July (Thurs). Proceeded via Porto Cabello (16th), LaGuaria (17th), Port of Spain, Trinidad (19th), Barbados (20th) and Madeira (28th) to Plymouth, arriving Plymouth 3.00am 31st (Sat). Landed 7.00am and proceeded to Sunderland, reporting Newcastle Depot am Aug 3rd. On leave Aug 4th - 11th (home 5th - 9th) standing by for appointment to S/S Goodwood - new collier (France Fenwicke) building at Austins yard Sunderland. **Signed on S/S Goodwood** (on board) Aug 11th (Wed). Ship now completed, and loading at Wearmouth Staithes [near Sunderland]."

S/S Goodwood
Built 1937
Gross Registered Tonnage 2796
Length 306 feet
Beam 45 feet
Horse Power 244: Steam driven piston engine.

S/S Goodwood 12 - 23 August 1937 [11 days] :

Wearmouth (near Sunderland, north-east England), London (discharged full cargo), Jarrow (loaded full cargo of coal), Antwerp (discharged full cargo), Dunstan on Tyne.

At Dunstan they loaded a full cargo of coal then, at 6.00am on 28th August, left on loaded trials. The trials were delayed by fog on the river. They anchored north of the Tyne entrance because fog was obscuring marks on the measured mile and they were waiting for it to clear. It didn't, so the trial was abandoned and they went to Wearmouth to land the trial party on a tug. They then proceeded on their voyage:

28 August - 9 September 1937 [12 days] :

Wearmouth (full cargo), London - Dagenham (discharged cargo), Pelaw - River Tyne (loaded full cargo of coal), Selzaete - Belgium (discharged cargo), back to Pelaw.

Last entry in the log

130

The log ends here. S/S Goodwood was Jack's last ship and his Certificate of Discharge shows that he left it at the completion of this voyage, on 9th September 1937.

The log, dispassionate as ever, says nothing about how he felt.

- Was he relieved to be moving on from a rather lonely life in cramped cabins?
- Was he sad that he would no longer travel round the world?
- Was he unsettled by leaving the familiar and embarking on a completely different life?
- Was he looking forward to the adventure of a new future?

He doesn't say. He never did say.

From what I unconsciously absorbed as I grew up, I think he had been contented at sea but was happy to move on. He had had enough travelling about. He was occasionally a little nostalgic, but long voyages away at sea didn't really go with married life. And he wanted to be married.

Jack had left the sea. He and Mercia married on 1 January 1938.

22. Landed

This isn't a biography but it seems abrupt to stop the story dead, just there. So I thought I should add a brief account of Jack and Mercia's ongoing voyage.

Nobody kept a diary. I've had to draw from things I remember being told and from things I remember directly.

April 1938

When they married, Jack and Mercia bought a semi-detached house in Barrow-in-Furness - twenty minutes or so by train from Jack's old home in Foxfield, where his parents still lived. It was rather more distant from Mercia's family, in Sunderland on the opposite side of the country.

It seems to me, looking back on it, that living in a semi in a small town must have been something of a contrast to their lives before.

There wasn't a big demand, away from the sea, for expertise in using morse code and making maritime radios work. So Jack joined his father in his small, home-based one-man (now two) business, making and selling medicines for farmers to use on their animals. Jack's father had trained as a chemist and made his own recipes of salves and the like, and he bought wholesale items to repackage and sell in retail amounts. It was all done in a small, rented shed near the rented house. The farmers spoke well of the medicines. They seemed to work and the farmers could treat their animals themselves without the expense of calling in a vet.

Jack wasn't needed full time in the business so he also worked part-time in a solicitors office in Broughton-in-Furness (about a mile from his parents in Foxfield), helping with the paperwork. As far as I know, Mercia didn't work. That was normal in those times.

In 1939 my brother, John, was born. Within a couple of weeks of that, the Second World War started. I'm sure there was no connection!

Jack was too old to be in the services so he joined the Home Guard.

Living in Barrow then became a problem. Vickers-Armstrong had a shipyard there, building war ships, so it was a target for bombs. Like many families, Jack and Mercia evacuated to the countryside to get away from that danger. I don't know the timing of it all but they ended up on a farm very near Foxfield. I was born there.

A few months later, Jack's father died. A nice man by all accounts, but I never knew him. Jack's mother continued to live in the same rented house and Jack ran the veterinary medicine business on his own from the shed.

They never returned to live in Barrow. After the war, they sold the house. Briefly they lived in Ulverston. Then they bought a house in the village of Kirkby-in-Furness, about five minutes by train from Jack's old home and the veterinary medicine shed.

Kirkby is the first place I remember. I went to the village school there, did villagey things and had villagey friends (we were little thugs as I remember it, all good fun).

There wasn't a lot of money. The seagoing savings had pretty much gone, probably helped by the war. There were no bottles of whisky (in fact it was a dry house), no outings to restaurants, pubs, theatres or cinemas. Just the "wireless" for entertainment, and the mobile library. The nearest I got to a holiday was to travel with Mercia, my mother, to see her family in Sunderland. Jack had done all the travelling he wanted. And he pointed out that if he took time off, his work would just pile up and be waiting for him when he got back. It was easier for him to just keep at it.

There was still food rationing after the war, so it was pretty healthy eating! For a few months, a sign of being a bit hard up, Mercia went back to nursing. She commuted on the train to Barrow and nursed in the hospital there. My brother by then was going to secondary school in Dalton, a significant bus ride away. So I was a latch-key kid. Aged eight or nine, I walked home from the village school and let myself into the empty house. I rather liked having the place to myself for an hour or two.

I also learned a life lesson when alone in the house. If you decided, when nobody was there to stop you, to treat yourself to a spoonful of delicious sugar, it was a good plan, I discovered, to make sure it wasn't a spoonful of salt! I've never forgotten that lesson! And it has analogies of all sorts.

We acquired a kitten who turned into a cat, as they do. Sometimes (especially if hungry) it was friendly. Sometimes it was aloof. Mostly, it was asleep. It joined us as a member of our self-contained, contented and rather isolated core family. We were all very fond of it.

To get around, Jack had his old Velocette motorbike. He rode it with some verve! There was a tramp who regularly visited the village. When Jack roared past him, the tramp always waved both arms wildly and shouted "Whizz on!"

Then, in 1953, several significant things happened. First, Jack got a new job, looking after three local branches of the National Farmers Union. It meant travelling round to farms, or being visited by farmers, to find out what their problems were and follow them up. It fitted in well with supplying veterinary medicines to them, so he kept that business going.

The new job needed a car. We got a car. Jack whizzed around in that, too. Occasionally, he would give one of the village wives a lift back from the shops. They would climb out of the car looking pale and in need of sweet tea.

The second thing to happen was rather sadder. Mercia's father died. He had lived to a good age so it wasn't a shock but it was still a loss. He was an enthusiastic, intelligent, likeable old bloke. He had been a successful businessman, ending up as a commercial coal merchant in Sunderland. His son, my uncle, inherited and ran the business, as was normal then. The daughters, including Mercia, inherited useful sums. It didn't make us rich but we were no longer hard up.

Shortly after that, my remaining grandparent, Jack's mother, died. That was sudden and unexpected but, again, she wasn't young.

The owners of the rented house she had lived in for nearly fifty years wanted to sell. Jack and Mercia bought it: Foxfield was a better location for Jack's new job. They sold the Kirkby house.

The new house was given a new kitchen, and running water in the back attic so the medicine making could be moved there. The shed became a garage for the car. Later, it also became a workshop.

In the middle of 1954 we moved to the newly bought house. This fitted neatly with my leaving the Kirkby village school and starting my first year at Ulverston Grammar School - with the delight of daily return journeys by stinky bus over twisty moorland roads.

The four of us, and the cat, settled in. There were no other kids living nearby so my brother, John, and I had to be self-sufficient. John, spent hours in the shed fixing bikes and, later, motorbikes. I got plans for a canoe and built it.

The canoe's keel had to be fixed to something firm while the frame was being built, so I screwed it to my bedroom floor. When finished, I spent many hours paddling my canoe around on the nearby estuary. I found that the quickest way between two points was often not direct. It depended on the tide and on invisible channels and currents underneath the surface. Another life lesson with lots of analogies.

All was calm. John left school and started working in Barrow shipyard, sprinting for the train every morning with a tenth of a second to spare. I continued my daily bus trips to school, thankfully having less motion sickness as I grew older.

The wireless was supplemented by a black and white television and a record playing radiogram.

During the school holidays I often went in the car with Jack, my Dad, visiting farmers. I was useful for opening and closing gates and we were good company for each other.

The first hiccup in our settled life was when Jack had a heart attack. It wasn't a bad one and he soon recovered. But it was a warning we didn't recognise.

A year later, I started the decline in our cohesion. I left home to be a university student. Older brother John, feeling a bit left out, also left home for a year. He went to sea as an engineer on a large passenger liner. It was very different to Jack's career at sea but got him round the world. He came back to work again in Barrow shipyard while I continued to live away as a student.

Then we had a great shock. Jack had a stroke. This time he didn't survive. Suddenly, he was gone. He and Mercia had been married just twenty-five years.

Mercia, widowed for the second time, lived on in the house for a few more years, out-surviving the cat. Brother John got married and moved out. I had never moved back in and was working in London.

Cancer struck. Mercia died. It happened swiftly and without notice, which was a comfort of sorts.

The house was sold.

Jack's compact family unit was no more. The last voyage had hit an iceberg and had foundered.

There remained some furniture, some bits and pieces and some photographs. And memories, of course.

And a hand-written log ...

End

- — —   - - - -   - -   — — - -   — — - -   — — —   — -

The Ships

The information about the ships in the table overleaf, also interspersed in the text, is from Lloyds Register of Shipping, accessed on-line. It uses the records digitised by Plimsoll for ships on register from 1930 - 1939.

Apart from two small tankers (MV British Union and SS Bachaquero), they were general cargo ships, except possibly the MacBrayne ships - RMS Clydesdale and RMS Lochbroom - which distributed mail and carried passengers round the Scottish West Coast and Islands.

By today's standards they were all small and not very powerful or fast.

With a few exceptions, the ships were coal fired with steam driven, triple expansion, piston engines. High pressure steam drove the high pressure cylinder; the steam leaving this expanded through the larger intermediate pressure cylinder and the steam leaving this, in turn, expanded through the even larger low pressure cylinder. The oldest ship, RMS Lochbroom, only had a double expansion engine (two cylinders).

The four Clan Line ships took the steam leaving the low pressure cylinder and expanded it further through a low pressure turbine, geared to the propeller shaft. Because of the higher rotational speed of a turbine, they also had direct reduction gearing from the turbine to the propeller shaft and they were fitted with a hydraulic coupling (so the turbine could be disengaged).

One ship (SS Cordillera) was entirely steam turbine driven.

All five ships with turbines (the Clans and Corderilla) were coal fired but had the option of burning oil.

MV British Union had a diesel engine, not steam, so needed oil fuel.

Bachaquero had twin screws, with each driven by its own steam engine, giving some backup in case of breakdown and more operating flexibility.

Not surprisingly, all these ships are described as having "Wireless".

Name [1]	Built	Tonnage (GRT [2])	Length & Beam (feet [3])
SS War Timiskaming	1919 Canada	?	?
SS Newquay	1914	4207	370 x 51
SS Massis	1914	5022	385 x 50
SS Gyp	1905	3338	340 x 48
SS Spilsby	1910	3673	347 x 51
SS Levenpool	1911	4844	376 x 57
SS Baron Forbes	1915 Germany	3061	303 x 43
SS Baron Garioch	1918	2508	303 x 43
RMS Clydesdale	1905	401	151 x 26
SS Dunrobin	1924 Glasgow	5041	405 x 53
SS Clan MacNair	1921	6096	411 x 53
SS Clan MacIlwraith	1924	4838	387 x 52
RMS Lochbroom	1871 Glasgow	1086	242 x 31
SS Cordillera	1920	6865	419 x 45
SS Clan MacIndoe	1920	4635	385 x 52
SS Baron Tweedsmouth	?	?	?
SS Homeside	1924	4617	384 x 52
SS Holtby	1909	3681	347 x 54
SS Fishpool	1912	4575	379 x 56
SS Euphorbia	1924	3380	331 x 48
SS Clan MacNab	1920	6117	411 x 53
MV British Union	1927	6987	440 x 57
SS Bachaquero	1937	4890	371 x 64
SS Goodwood	1937	2796	306 x 45

1   SS = Steam Ship
    RMS = Royal Mail Ship (these two are also steam ships)
    MV = Motor Vessel (i.e diesel engine, not steam)
2   Gross Registered Tons (GRT) relates to volume, not actual weight. It is the number of units of 100 cubic feet (about 2.7 cubic metres) which will fit into the useable internal space.
3   For those who prefer metres, 1 foot (ft) = 0.305 metres.
    eg SS Baron Garioch was 92 metres long and 13 metres wide.

Power Units and Voyage Areas

Power (HP [4])	Boiler Pressure (psi [5])	Other Notes on Ships	Main Areas visited and recorded in the Log
?	?		*Canada (East Coast)*
386	180		*Mediterranean Sea [Med]*
425	180		*Med, USA, Asia, Australia*
308	180		*Canada, Med, Netherlands*
96	80		*Med, USA, Cuba, Scandinavia*
442	180		*Canada, USA, Netherlands*
253	185	ex SS Napier	*Med*
217	?		*Med, Canada, USA, Cuba, Iceland*
85	?	MacBrayne	*Scottish West Coast*
410	180		*Med, USA, Cuba, S. America*
639	200	Clan Line	*Med, Africa, India &Ceylon*
653	180	Clan Line	*Med, India*
262	70	MacBrayne	*Scottish West Coast*
756	200	all turbine	*W. Africa, S. America, Australia*
613	180	Clan Line	*India*
?	?		*British coast - very brief*
406	180		*South America*
301	?		*Canada*
380	180		*Canada, Netherlands*
249	?		*USA, Cuba*
692	200	Clan Line	*USA, Africa, India*
749	n/a	6cyl diesel	*Scandinavia*
551	225	twin screw	*South America*
244	220		*Belgium - brief*

4   Horse Power (HP) refers to the power available at the
    screw (propellor). 1 HP is about 0.75 kilowatts. For
    comparison, a modern inter-city bus might have an
    engine of around 300 HP.

5   Pounds per square inch (psi). Atmospheric pressure is
    about 15 psi so most of these ships have steam pressure
    around 12 to 15 atmospheres. A modern power station
    team pressure is around 2400 psi (160 atmospheres).

Meanings and Measures

A few nautical terms, abbreviations and conventions appear in the log. Some are well known or obvious, included here anyway for completeness (and in case they are not known or obvious to you!) and some amount to jargon. I've listed them more or less in alphabetical order.

Abeam: to the side of the ship. Or *beam on* to it.

Aft, After or *Stern* refer to the back of the ship.

Beam: the width of the ship. **Beam on** means *abeam* of it.

Bow: The front, pointed end of the ship. At the *fore* end.

Bunkers means fuel, nearly always coal in these vessels. The convention was for coal fuel to be loaded into a sort of hopper (bunker) within the ship and for stokers to take it from the bottom. So Taking on Bunkers or Calling for Bunkers means refuelling. It was still the term used when taking on oil fuel.

Case-oil a term used for petrol, paraffin etc. carried in drums.

Swinging the **compass**: Magnetic compasses are deflected by magnetism in the metal of the ship and the deflection changes over time. So they swing the ship through a full circle noting the position of known landmarks, and prepare a deviation chart to adjust compass readings to actual bearings.

Draft is how far down the ship projects into the water below the waterline. Obviously, it needs at least that much depth, plus a bit of clearance, to avoid going aground.

Fathom. Depth of water is usually measured in fathoms. It's a thousandth of a nautical mile, about six feet (1.8 metres).

Feet (ft or ') and Inches (ins or "). Still widely used as measures of length, of course, but not so much in countries which have gone metric. 12" = 1'. A foot is about 0.305 metres. Inches only appear in this book in relation to engine component dimensions: 24" is about 0.6 metres.

Fore or Forrard: towards the front of the ship.

Forecastle: the front deck of the ship.

Great Britain: The biggest island of the British Isles - the one with England, Scotland and Wales on it.

Gross registered tonnage (grt) of a ship is not its weight on a big weighing scale but is the ship's enclosed, useable internal volume in units of 100 cubic feet (about 2.7 cubic metres). Jack's ships typically had grt of 3000 to 5000 - pretty small by today's standards.   (The liner, Queen Mary 2, admittedly big, has a grt of 150000).

Heaving to, or being **hove to**, means the ship is not trying to make progress but is moving only enough to steer and minimise the impact of heavy seas and high winds in a storm.

Kedge or **Kedge Anchor** – an anchor placed well to the stern of the vessel to hold it off the shore or to help haul it off the shore if it has grounded. (It's a tautology to say a kedge anchor was put out aft or from the stern).

Knot. A measure of speed. A speed of 1 knot is 1 *nautical mile* per hour (1.85 Km/hr). Most of these ships would have travelled at around 8 - 10 knots (15 - 18 km/hr) most of the time. Not fast by car standards (still less, aircraft) but they kept it up all day and every day.

Lee, Leeward, In the Lee of: Downwind, so sheltered.

A **Lighter** is an open, shallow draft barge used to ferry cargo to and from shore if the ship was unable to tie up directly to a wharf. It involved double handling of the cargo so using lighters is inefficient, but it was very common.

Light ship usually means travelling with no cargo in this context. Of course, a "light ship" can also mean an anchored vessel with a light on it, aiding navigation. But see...

Light Vessel (LV). An anchored vessel with a light on it, aiding navigation.

£.s.d. British money before 1971 when it was decimalised. £ means a pound; s was a shilling and d was an (old) penny. 12 pennies = 1 shilling. 20 shillings = 1 pound. Abbreviated, 3/4, for example, meant 3 shillings and 4 pence. On decimalisation, Britain kept the pound but divided it into 100p: p is a (new) penny.

Marconi Man. The Marconi Company was the employer for the *Wireless Telegraphy Operators* provided to shipping lines, and so, informally, known as Marconi Men.

Mile. In this context, a mile means a *nautical mile* –about 6000 feet (or 1850 metres or 1.85 kilometres). Its origin is as a minute of arc round the earth's circumference.

Morse Code. See next section (page 147). A code to represent letters of the alphabet, and numbers, by a series of short dots and longer dashes, originally used in telegraphs.

MV means Motor Vessel. It has a diesel engine, rather than being an *SS* or *Steam Ship*. There is no obvious reason why the convention is to call it a Vessel rather than a Ship.

Nautical Mile. See *Mile.*

Poop or Poop Deck: the deck above the *stern.*

Port and **Starboard** are left and right when looking forwards (towards the *Bow*). Of course, Port also means a harbour with all the usual facilities for ships.

RMS means Royal Mail Ship: a ship which delivered the mail within or to and from Britain. Typically a ship with a regular service schedule, not a jobbing transport at call. In the log, Carmania - the Cunard transatlantic liner - and Clydesdale and Lochbroom - which ran regular services around the west coast of Scotland - were Royal Mail Ships.

Roads: A relatively sheltered and current-free area of water where ships can safely anchor, often near a port.

Satnav: Satellite Navigation, which they certainly didn't have back then, so navigation was more of a challenge.

S/S means steam ship, which they nearly all were. Jack adopted the convention of separating the S's with a slash, so I stuck with it.

Stern: *Aft* or back of the ship.

Stood off and on means that, for some reason, they couldn't finalise arriving at a destination and couldn't anchor so they just pottered to and fro until the situation was resolved.

Trials: with a new ship, or after significant upgrades or modifications, it's normal for it to be tested to make sure it works –and specifically to see how fast it will go. They had markers on shore a (nautical) mile apart and timed their transit between them. These days *Satnav* will do it.

Wireless Telegraphy (W/T) means sending and receiving messages by radio, usually in *Morse Code.*

Wireless Telegraphy Operator (WTO) - the officer who sends and receives messages and keeps the equipment in working order.

Morse Code

Samuel Morse was a man of talents. An American who spent some time in Britain, he had an established career as a portrait painter. In the 1800s he turned his attention to invention, specifically pushing for the establishment of long distance telegraph communication, by wire.

In addition to the technology and infrastructure, this needed a code to represent letters and numbers. He established the Morse Code of dots and dashes to do this.

The Code was widely used and became the standard for communication at sea until newer technologies made it redundant. Here are the codes for letters:

A	▪ ▬		N	▬ ▪
B	▬ ▪ ▪ ▪		O	▬ ▬ ▬
C	▬ ▪ ▬ ▪		P	▪ ▬ ▬ ▪
D	▬ ▪ ▪		Q	▬ ▬ ▪ ▬
E	▪		R	▪ ▬ ▪
F	▪ ▪ ▬ ▪		S	▪ ▪ ▪
G	▬ ▬ ▪		T	▬
H	▪ ▪ ▪ ▪		U	▪ ▪ ▬
I	▪ ▪		V	▪ ▪ ▪ ▬
J	▪ ▬ ▬ ▬		W	▪ ▬ ▬
K	▬ ▪ ▬		X	▬ ▪ ▪ ▬
L	▪ ▬ ▪ ▪		Y	▬ ▪ ▬ ▬
M	▬ ▬		Z	▬ ▬ ▪ ▪

The sender used a "key" - a sensitive, sprung switch with a knob on it - operated by hand to transmit short dots and longer dashes. The receiver listened to the incoming sequence of dots and dashes and wrote down the letters (and numbers) by hand, to form the message.

Speed of sending and receiving was important, so Wireless Telegraphy Operators, like Jack, had to meet specified speeds in order to qualify. Translating between letters (and numbers) and the code had to become automatic: there wasn't time to think.

The influence of the code still lives on. The international distress signal in Morse was the easily remembered three dots, three dashes, three dots. It translates to SOS and that's still a common saying for an emergency or a call for help in our everyday language. SOS is usually said to mean "Save Our Souls" but this was probably an afterthought. The convention really originated with the simplicity and memorability of the Morse signal.

More recently, the default sound on some mobile phones (originally Nokia, I think) for a text message being received goes: dit dit dit dah dah dit dit dit. Morse for SMS, or Short Message Service - the official name for a text.

www.ingramcontent.com/pod-product-compliance
Lightning Source LLC
Chambersburg PA
CBHW051042030426
42339CB00006B/151